Negotiating the Thousand Glories

OrangeBooks Publication

1st Floor, Rajhans Arcade, Mall Road, Kohka, Bhilai, Chhattisgarh 490020

Website: **www.orangebooks.in**

First Edition, 2024

NEGOTIATING THE THOUSAND GLORIES

ASHOK WARRIER

OrangeBooks Publication
www.orangebooks.in

Dedicated to all Seekers of
The Self within

Reviews

'Negotiating the Thousand Glories' by Ambassador Ashok Warrier is a glorious exposition of the significance both physical and spiritual of each and every name of Vishnu out of His thousand names in Vishnu Sahasranama. The author very lucidly and insightfully analyses the use of the cosmic power of Vishnu at all times and in every age to ensure the triumph of the forces of truth over untruth, of light over darkness, of immortality over mortality. I hail the author for bringing home that truth to everyone - to those who recite it every day and those who know little about this treatise of ancient vintage.

Ambassador Lakhan Mehrotra

In ancient Indian epistemology, Vedic culture and learning, whence various aspects of Hinduism emerged, the reality of Para and Apara vidya is paramount. Both branches of knowledge played a vital role in the education of human beings. Apara taught us about the phenomenal world of Physics and Mathematics; Para led us into the Absolute world, free of the senses!

To this spiritual world of knowledge, which is intuitive and believed to have been revealed to meditating Rishis from the Unknown, belongs the Vishnu Sahasranama (The Thousand Names of Vishnu). Vedanta texts like the Upanishads, the Gita, the Mandalas of Guru Vashistha belong in this genre. While these have been widely translated and disseminated by Vedantic missionaries globally, the Vishnu Sahasranama is not always on the same bookshelves or lecterns.

And yet the Sahasras contain the seeds from which burst forth the Para vidya of say, the Katha Upanishad or the Bhagwad Purana.

Author Ashok Warrier's 'Negotiating the Thousand Glories' comes as an important and unique addition to the growing body of the English translations of the texts of ancient Indian wisdom which are growing increasingly relevant in an existentially troubled, violent and spiritually maladjusted world.

Warrier, a seasoned and widely travelled former senior India diplomat who served as Ambassador to Congo, rightly sees that an increasingly schizophrenic world society, including India, in search of answers, needs only to turn to wisdom traditions preserved in texts like the Vishnu Sahasranama.

And Warrier has now made this task easier and within reach with 'Negotiating The Thousand Glories' in which you will read not only simplified accurate translations of the power - packed shlokas but also penetrating anecdotes and contextual explanations.

Warrier's work is a labour of love on par with Juan Mascaro's brilliant translation and interpretation of the Upanishads. His book is a must-read for all those across the world seeking paths to a spiritual journey.

Inderjit Badhwar (Prize -winning Author)
(Editor-in-Chief, India Legal Magazine; Former Chief Editor, India Today)

Preface

Dear Friends and Fellow Seekers,

As a child, I remember watching my mother chanting some shlokas. When I asked her what she was chanting, she told me that she was chanting the thousand names of Vishnu. Many years later, when I had grown up enough to realise the importance of words and their meanings, I asked her whether she knew the meanings of the names that she was chanting. She told me that she knew the names by heart but not the meanings. Later, I found that my mother was no exception. There are many people who know the thousand names of Lord Vishnu by heart, but there are very few who know the meanings of these names. I myself was one who has been chanting the Vishnu Sahasranama without really understanding the full importance and meaning of these shlokas. As I attempted to understand the meanings, it started becoming clearer to me that a recital of the shlokas with a better understanding of what they mean (even with the constraints and giving allowance to translations from Sanskrit to English) gave an entirely different perspective to both chanting and listening to the Vishnu Sahasranama. To put it simply, it gave the whole exercise a better sense of purpose. This thus has been my objective in writing this book. Hopefully, through this book, people like me who have been chanting the Vishnu Sahasranama or people (and here I include even children) who are getting to read it for the first time or trying to understand it better will be encouraged to pick up this book and go through it.

Translations can always be tricky as they may not necessarily capture the full or true meaning of a word or phrase. The Vishnu Sahasranama is largely a narrative of the attributes and names of Lord Vishnu, but then, it is not just that. There are subtle meanings attached to most words and verses. Hence, one often finds that for every word or phrase, there is a literal meaning and also one or even several metaphysical or philosophical meanings. I would illustrate this point with three examples:

Let us take the following Shloka (Stanza 5 of the Vishnu Sahasranama):

svayambhūś śambhurādityaf
pushkarāksho mahāsvanaha |
anādinidhano dhātā
vidhātā dhāturuttamaha ||

The word '*Aadityah*' refers to the Truth that glows with a golden splendour in the solar orbit. There are 12 such *Aadityahs,* and Lord Vishnu is one of them. Lord Krishna himself declares in the Bhagavad Gita: 'I am Vishnu among the Aadityas'. However, this is not the only meaning of Aadityah. *Aadityah* can be the 'son of Aditi', born as a *Vaamana* in one of Lord Vishnu's incarnations. '*Aadityah*' can again also mean 'One who is like the Sun', which illuminates everything in this Universe.

Let us now take an example in Shloka 15:

lokādhyakshas surādhyaksho
dharmādhyakshah kṛtākṛtaha |
chaturātmā chatur-vyūhaś
chaturdamshṭraś chaturbhujaha ||

The word '*Chaturbhujaha*' literally means 'One who has four arms'. However, going beyond, the arms have a conch (*Shankh*), Mace (*Gada*), Discus (*Chakra*) and a Lotus (*Padma*), respectively. According to the Puranas, these four are used by the Lord to maintain Dharma or Righteousness. The sound from the conch *(Panchajanya)* is the voice of conscience meant to steer us along the path of virtue; ignoring it would mean the use of the mace by the Lord and facing certain hurdles and challenges by way of punishment; continued defiance would invoke the use of the Chakra and annihilation - all of these are meant to get us to the Ultimate Goal represented by the Lotus.

Let us now take the example of Stanza 97:

araudrah kuṇḍalī chakrī
***vikramyūrjitaśāsanaha* |**
śabdātigaś śabdasahaś
***śiśiraś śarvarīkaraha* ||**

Here, if we were to take the word '*Kundali*', it would simply mean 'the wearer of earrings' (Literal meaning). But it could also mean

'Serpent' which, in turn, could refer to the 'Mind' (Metaphysical meaning). Lord Vishnu is visualised as reclining on the thousand tongued serpent, Anantha - a symbolic representation of His having conquered the Mind denoted by the poisonous serpent lying coiled within the body.

Addressing all the meanings and interpretations and sifting through the nuanced differences in them is quite frankly beyond my capabilities, given my extremely limited understanding of the original language (Sanskrit). For this, there are very eminent and erudite scholars who have brought out copious commentaries on the Vishnu Sahasranama.

I have generally and largely confined myself to the simple meanings (without delving too deep) of the shlokas while narrating some anecdotal stories and context for the circumstances, attributes and characters involved or mentioned in the Vishnu Sahasranama.

While there are three defined paths in Hinduism of seeking and attaining Moksha or liberation from the cycle of births and deaths, namely through Karma or action, Jnana or knowledge and Bhakti or devotion, it is not that these paths are independent of each other.

However, there could always be a preponderance of one over the other(s). The battlefield of Kurukshetra itself sees an exhortation of two types of yoga: karma yoga by Krishna to Arjuna and bhakti yoga by Bhishma to Yudhishthira. While Krishna's core message in the Bhagavad Gita (or the 'Song of the Lord') to Arjuna was an exhortation to action, viz. to carry out his duty as a Kshatriya or warrior without being weighed down by sentiments and emotions or for that matter the nature of the results, Bhishma's message to Yudhishthira was to practise intense devotion to Lord Vishnu in order to administer his Kingdom well with fairness and justice. Both were messages laced with practical wisdom and designed to reach the ultimate goal of Moksha. Although Bhishma recites to Yudhisthira the thousand names of Lord Vishnu and exhorts him to chant them on a daily basis with intense bhakti or devotion, let us not forget that both Bhishma, the giver of the message and Yudhisthira, the receiver of the message were men of wisdom 'Jnanis' themselves. They both had only very recently fought in the great Mahabharata War in keeping with their calling as 'Kshatriyas', which made both of them Karma yogis too. This further reaffirms that no path to salvation is mutually exclusive of each other - a learning that we all can bear in mind as we go along facing challenges in today's increasingly complex world!

Vishnu Sahasranama brings out in full measure the munificence and understanding of Lord Vishnu towards his devotees. In one of the Shlokas in the Phalashruti, Krishna, in response to a plea by his friend, Arjuna, tells him that he will be happy and content if a devotee is to chant even as much as one shloka with sincerity. Again, one of the most abiding aspects which comes out is the theme of Universal values. The prayers, too, are never for oneself but for humanity at large. In the Phalashruti, Arjuna, for instance, pleads for Krishna's understanding and compassion for all his devotees. In today's times of fractiousness, discordance in society often exacerbated by social media and the like, anger and acrimony, diminishing understanding and patience, this great work of Veda Vyasa can be a calming lodestar, the need for which we all have felt, at some point of time or the other. Therefore, the Vishnu Sahasranama has not without reason been termed as one of the '*ratnas*' or jewels of the Mahabharata!!

This book is not and can never be a compendium on the Vishnu Sahasranama but is a very modest attempt to make it as simple (and hopefully interesting too) as possible so as to enable all those (including children as I had mentioned earlier) who are interested to follow and understand this most abiding work composed by a truly exceptional genius (Veda Vyasa), and narrated by one of the most ardent devotees of Lord Vishnu (Bhishma) to one of the most virtuous and upright men of his generation (Yudhisthira).

I would like to place on record my sense of deep appreciation and thanks to Mrs Rajalakshmi Sathiapalan, a well-read person who has extensive discussions with her like-minded friends on subjects like Advaita Vedanta, Vishnu Sahasranama, Narayaneeyam and Bhagvatam; her physicist son, Dr Balachandran Sathiapalan, who takes a keen interest in Indian philosophy. Both mother and son are very conversant with Sanskrit language and have a deep interest in the same. They both have gone through the manuscript with much care. I would also like to place on record my profound thanks to Dr Binoo Nayar, an Eye surgeon by profession and a keen chanter of Vishnu Sahasranama, who has put her sharp eyes to pore over my manuscript in great detail. All three of them have given some extremely valuable insights and suggestions that have found their way into this book. And of course, I cannot thank my life partner, Sunita, enough for undertaking the bulk of the typing, providing some useful tips and always being available to help me when required.

I hope you enjoy this book and also indulge me as a seeker, learning the ropes for any of the errors, factual or otherwise, that might have crept in.

Ashok Warrier

April, 2024

Contents

Chapter - 1

Pūrvāngam: The First Part

Pūrvāngam is the synthesis of two Sanskrit words namely, Pūrvā and Angam in which Pūrvā, in the context in which it appears here, means 'earlier one' or 'former' while 'Angam' refers to the main 'body'. Pūrvāngam thus refers to the verses which herald the main Vishnu Sahasranama. It is an introduction to the glories of Lord Vishnu; the lineage of the author, Veda Vyasa, as also a grateful recognition and acknowledgement of his genius and the 6 questions posed by Yudhisthira, the newly anointed King of Hastinapura to Bhishma, the grand old man of the epic, Mahabharata and the responses given by him.

The architecture: Vishnu Sahasranama essentially means the thousand names of Lord Vishnu spread over 108 slokas. Each shloka is arranged along 4 lines and has 16 syllables. But why 108, one might ask? Is it a random number, or is there a basis for it?

All about alignment: According to Vedic studies on cosmology, the number 108 is the very basis of creation. Yogic scholars and practitioners of the Siddha form of medicine had worked out even as far as then that the human body has within it 108 pressure points or 'chakras' and that every mantra or shloka needed to be chanted 108 times in order to activate all the chakras. Vedic astronomers and mathematicians had discovered and computed that the distance between the Sun and the Earth and that between the Moon and the Earth was 108 times the diameter of the Sun and the Moon, respectively.

The location of the Earth is such that both the Sun and the Moon appear to be of the same size as seen from the Earth. This becomes even more evident during phenomena like total solar eclipse when the moon completely and totally covers the

Sun. What does all this tell us? **It basically tells us that the scholars of the Vedic times recognised the need to align the human body to cosmic geometry.**

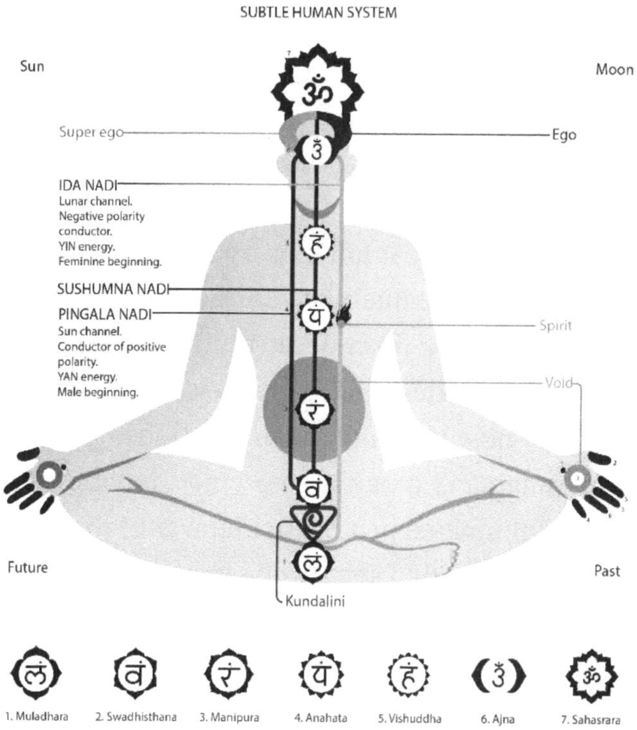

Human body and chakras

One can only marvel at the wisdom and knowledge of these scholars! This knowledge also explains the overwhelming presence of the number 108 in many of the Hindu practices. The sanctity of this number having been recognised and established, all mantras and slokas were set to this number and Vishnu Sahasranama was no exception. It is also no surprise, therefore, to have 108 Upanishads - spiritual and philosophical texts, 108 Ganas or attendants of Lord Shiva, 108 beads, 108 Gopis in Vrindavan, 108 forms of meditation, and so many 108s more!

Gems in the Garland: Let us now get back to the *nāmas* or names of Lord Vishnu. These names are in the form of attributes, epithets and qualities that describe Lord Vishnu's various aspects, powers and manifestations. Vishnu Sahasranama is a part of the epic Mahabharata, which culminated in a fratricidal war of the same name between two sets of cousins, the Kauravas and the Pandavas. The epic itself contains five '*ratnas*' or gems. These figure as various '*Parvas*' of the epic in the form of dialogues or conversations.

The first one is in the form of a conversation between Dhritarashtra, the blind King and father of the Kauravas and Vidura, his half-brother known as Viduraneeti. The second one is a conversation between Dhritarashtra and the Sanat Kumaraas (sons of Lord Brahma) known as Sanatsujaatheeyam; the third one is between Yudhishthira, the eldest of the Pandava princes, and Yaksha, who came in disguise as a questioner, known as Yakshaprashnam; the fourth one is between Krishna (incarnation of Lord Vishnu) and Arjuna, his close friend and admirer, very well known as the Bhagavad Gita and finally, there is the conversation between Bhishma, the oldest member of the Bharata clan (the ancestral lineage of the Kauravas and Pandavas) and the one fondly and reverentially referred to as the Pitamah (grandfather of the Kauravas and Pandavas) and Yudhisthira, the eldest of the Pandava princes and the new King of Hastinapura, known as the Vishnu Sahashranama.

Conversations on the battlefield:

The Mahabharata war was fought in Kurukshetra, which is presently located in the state of Haryana. Kurukshetra was not just a battleground for the War, but also the place where **two most profound conversations** (namely, the fourth and the fifth referred to above) took place. These conversations were simple and natural yet very deep and profound, carrying a message both of practical wisdom and life lessons for humanity at large, which is why the battlefield of Kurukshetra (the area or place belonging to the Kuru clan) came to be known as '*Dharmakshetra*' (the area or place where the Cosmic Law was upheld) too. The first conversation was before the commencement of the War, before the first arrow was even shot, and the second one was after the war was over when there was perhaps no arrow left to be shot. The one before the commencement of the War was **between Krishna, the mentor and his protégé, Arjuna and is known as the Bhagavad Gita**, a treatise on manifold aspects of life, including the discharge of one's duties irrespective of results. The second conversation was **between Bhishma, the Pitamaha, and Yudhisthira, the eldest of the Pandavas, who is also now the King of Hastinapura, and it is this that is known as Vishnu Sahasranama** or the Thousand Names (Sahasranama) of Lord Vishnu.

The Quandary-Stricken King:

The Mahabharata War is over. Yudhisthira is crowned as the King. But he is not a happy man. He feels that he himself is responsible for the war and its consequences. The loss of his near and dear ones, including all the children of the Pandavas, his own teachers and well-wishers, is tormenting him. He is sad, morose and confused. He approaches Krishna and shares his feelings with Him. Krishna suggests that all the Pandavas should go to the battlefield, pay respects to Bhishma and Yudhisthira should seek his advice on how to move forward in life.

Krishna further tells Yudhisthira that they should visit Bhishma before Uttarayana when Bhishma would be leaving his body. (Bhishma had been conferred a boon of *ichhamrityu* by his father meaning that he could himself choose the time to leave his body). All the Pandavas, accompanied by Draupadi and Krishna, accordingly go to the battlefield and stand before Bhishma, who is lying on a bed of arrows made by his grandson Arjuna.

Uttarayana: But why was Bhishma waiting for Uttarayana to leave his body? What was so special about Uttarayana? The word Uttarayana is a synthesis of the words '*Uttara*' meaning North, and '*Ayana*' meaning movement, which refers to the apparent northward movement of the Sun. The revolution of the Earth around the Sun and its tilted axis is what makes the Sun appear as moving northwards from the Tropic of Capricorn to the Tropic of Cancer in the Northern Hemisphere. During Uttarayana, the days gradually become longer over a period of six months, with nights becoming shorter in the Northern Hemisphere, which is where India and the battlefield of Kurukshetra are located. This period is believed to be the most auspicious one as it is also the daytime for the Devas or Gods, which is why most weddings and auspicious events are scheduled during this period. It also ushers in the harvest season across India and the auspicious Makara Sankranti (known by various other names across India like Bihu in Assam, Pongal in Tamil Nadu, Makara Vilakku in Kerala, Uttarayan in Gujarat, Poush Sankranti in Bengal etc.), when the Sun God or Surya Dev is worshipped by the Hindus, falls during this period. Let us not forget that the date and time chosen for the historic Pran Prathishta (infusing life force into the deity) of Ram Lalla (the 5-year-old Sri Rama) in Ayodhya was again carried out during the Uttarayana period on January 22, 2024. The period of Uttarayana is considered to be the most auspicious, as well as for one to shed the body and attain *moksha* or liberation from the cycle of birth and rebirth. In fact, the moksha aspect of the Uttarayana is mentioned in the Bhagavad Gita, where Lord Krishna expounds on this to Arjuna. So, it is no surprise to have the great Bhishma continuing to lie on the bed of arrows and awaiting his soul to leave his mortal body till the advent of Uttarayana!

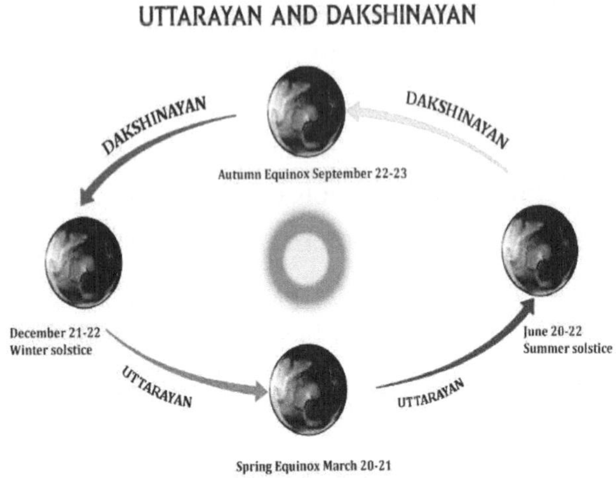

Geographical illustration of Uttarayana

Draupadi's ire and Bhishma's response: Coming back to the visit of Draupadi, Krishna and the Pandavas to the battlefield, it is mentioned that Draupadi was still smarting under the humiliation she suffered in the open court, where Dushasana, the brother of Duryodhana, the eldest of the Kaurava princes, dragged her to the court, and tried to disrobe her in front of all the assembled elders and courtiers in the court of Hastinapura. She was looking up to the elders in the court, especially the most revered elder amongst them all, Bhishma, to come to her rescue. But the great Bhishma only showed helplessness. The fact that Bhishma did not or could not prevent this humiliation rankled in Draupadi's mind. She wanted to know from Yudhisthira as to why they should seek any advice at all from a person such as Bhishma, who could not prevent what happened in the court that day. Bhishma, who heard this, replied: "Yes child, you are well within your right to feel aggrieved. As the eldest member of the Bharata clan, I was obligated and pledged to protect the sovereignty and integrity of the Kingdom of Hastinapura. I was fully aware of the vile deeds being committed by Duryodhana, his brothers and friends. I was also aware of the indifference shown by Dhritarashtra and his blind love for his eldest son, Duryodhana.

But because of my obligation and pledge to always stand by the Kingdom of Hastinapura, I could not do anything. I was also consuming the salt of Dhritarashtra and his son, Duryodhana. But now that every single drop of that guilt-soaked blood has been drained out from my body, and as I lie here waiting for my death, I have no more obligations. Hence, what I shall say now will be the absolute truth and spoken with complete honesty." After these words, coming from the grcat Bhishma, there was nothing more for anyone to say!!

The grandfather warrior: Let us now know a little more about Bhishma. His actual name was Devavrata. 'Bhishma' was a title he acquired because of the terrible sacrificial vow he took. We shall shortly learn about the vow and the circumstances of the same. Bhishma was the elder brother of the grandfather of the Kauravas and Pandavas, and for this reason, he was termed as Pitamah or grandfather by both the Kauravas and Pandavas. As per the Bhagavad Purana, there are 12 *Mahajanas*. A *Mahajana* is an authority on the Vedas and on the art of self-realisation. **Bhishma was one such *Mahajana***. The others were Lord Brahma, Lord Shiva, Narada, the four Kumaras, Manu, Bali, Yama, Janaka, Prahlada, Sukadeva, and Kapila.

The terrible vow: Bhishma was the son of King Shantanu and Goddess Ganga. Goddess Ganga left King Shantanu after he broke a promise given to her. Later, the King fell in love with a fisherwoman, Satyawati. In order to allay the fears and concerns of Satyawati and her father, Bhishma, who was the rightful heir to the throne (being the son of King Shantanu from Goddess Ganga), promised the father and daughter that he would not only ***not*** stake a claim to the throne but will also remain celibate and committed to selflessly safeguarding the sovereignty of the kingdom of Hastinapura. **He thus sacrificed his claim to the throne and also pledged himself never to marry for the sake of his father, King Shantanu, and for his vow, he came to be known to the world as 'Bhishma'**. His father bestowed upon his son, Bhishma, a boon by which he could choose his own time of death (referred to earlier). Before we proceed any further, it may be noted that Bhishma was an ardent devotee of Lord Vishnu, whose avatar during the Mahabharata war was none other than Krishna himself, a fact very well known to Bhishma. There is an interesting story related to this. The war was raging and Bhishma proved to be more than a match for Arjuna. Krishna knew, more than perhaps anybody else, that if the Pandavas had to win the war, it was very important to vanquish Bhishma. Seeing that the battle between the grandfather and the grandson was not going anywhere, Krishna, in one of those rarest of rare moments, got angry, jumped out of the chariot that he was driving, picked up one of the chariot wheels lying around and menacingly advanced towards Bhishma. What did the great Bhishma do?

He simply dropped all his arms, broke into a broad smile and welcomed Krishna with the words, 'Vasudeva, I have all along been waiting for this moment. Is there a better way to kiss death than from the blessed hands of the great Krishna?' Arjuna, however, was aghast at the turn of events, ran after his friend Krishna and stopped him from executing his threat by reminding him of his solemn vow not to take up arms during the war. Arjuna also assured Krishna that he would do all he could to intensify the fight and vanquish Bhishma. It was after this that Krishna was pacified and got back to his chariot. This anecdote brings out the enormous respect, regard, admiration and devotion that Bhishma had for Krishna for whom He was none other than the omnipotent, omniscient Lord Vishnu. It also puts into context the narration of the Vishnu Sahasranama by Bhishma to Yudhisthira.

Bhishma Uttering The Terrible Vow

Conversation Between an Ardent Devotee and a Tormented King:

After offering his salutations to Bhishma, what follows was a conversation or rather a set of Q&A between Yudhisthira and Bhishma (recorded and registered in Anushasana Parva - the book of Instructions) wherein Bhishma in response to the **6 questions** (the questions have been numbered in the shlokas below) posed by Yudhisthira urged him to chant the 1000 names of Lord Vishnu or Vishnu Sahasranama composed by Sri Veda Vyasa. It may be worth noting here that the two main characters involved in the conversation, viz. Yudhisthira and Bhishma were undoubtedly two of the wisest men of their generation. Yudhisthira had so beautifully and brilliantly tackled and responded to all the 120 odd complex questions posed by Yaksha (please refer to the Yaksha Prashnam referred to in the 'Gems in the Garland') and brought back to life all his four siblings. As for Bhishma, he was, as already mentioned, one of the 12 *Mahajanas* and an extremely evolved soul. It may be noted that the Vishnu Sahasranama was recited by Bhishma to Yudhisthira not from the comfort of his palace quarters but while lying on a bed of sharp and pointed arrows piercing through his body into his very bones in a battlefield where the blood from the bodies of warriors, horses and elephants was yet to dry and get soaked up by the earth below. It was almost as if there was neither pain nor suffering for Bhishma but only the sheer ecstasy of devotional chanting of the Vishnu Sahasranama. This is what bhakti or devotion is all about.

There are innumerable instances of how ardent devotees have self-'realised' through the medium of *bhakti* and have been protected and blessed by Lord Vishnu. Prahlada was protected by Lord Vishnu, appearing as Narasimha avatar (face of a lion and body of a man), just as Draupadi was protected by Lord Vishnu in the form of Krishna. Krishna fully recognised the merit and worth of Bhishma. There is a story wherein after the war, while Krishna and his consort, Rukmini, are seated in Dwarka, Krishna's abode, Rukmini notices a tear streaming down the cheeks of Krishna. She is astonished to see this and asks him, 'Oh Krishna, you who makes people laugh and cry, why is it that I see the same Krishna now crying himself?' Krishna replies: 'Uttarayana is approaching and the great Bhishma will shortly be leaving his body. I will sorely miss his presence as there are not too many wise men like him left. His impending loss makes me sad.'

Getting back to the conversation, Bhishma tells Yudhisthira that regular chanting of the Vishnu Sahasranama will not only guide him in discharging his duties as a King but also ensure salvation from the constant cycle of birth and rebirth.

Since Krishna, who was none other than Lord Vishnu, was present when the conversation between Bhishma and Yudhishtira was happening, it is believed that the Lord will always be **present** when His names are being chanted. Going forward, let us see what the Pūrvāngam has to say:

śuklāmbaradharam vishṇum
śaśivarṇam chaturbhujam |
prasanna-vadanam dhyāyet
sarvavighnopa-śāntaye || (1) ||

Dressed in white, Oh, all-pervading ONE, glowing with the colour of the Moon, with four arms, You are the all-knowing ONE! I meditate on your ever-smiling face, and pray that you remove all obstacles in my way and usher in peace and calmness.

Lord Vishnu lying on the Adishesha

vyāsam vasishṭha naptāram
śaktef pautrama-kalmasham |
parāśarātmajam vande
śukatātam taponidhim || (2) ||

This shloka is an obeisance to Vyasa, who is the great grandson of Vashistha and the grandson of Shakti. He is the son of Parasara and the father of Suka. I offer my obeisance to that Vyasa, who is free from all defects and is a repository of austerities.

vyāsāya vishṇu rūpāya
vyāsarūpāya vishṇave |
namo vai brahma nidhaye
vāsishṭhāya namo namaha || (3) ||

My respected salutations to that Vyasa who is the form of Vishnu, and to Vishnu who is a form of Vyasa. My obeisance to Sage Vyasa who is a descendant of Vashishta and who is a treasure house of the knowledge of the Brahman.

Sage Vyasa sitting in meditation

avikārāya śuddhāya
nityāya paramātmane |
sadaika rūpa rūpāya
vishṇave sarvajishṇave || (4) ||

My obeisance to Vishnu, who is changeless, pure and eternal; whose form is immutable and constant and who is ever victorious.

yasya smaraṇa-mātreṇa
janma-samsāra-bandhanāt |
vimuchyate namastasmai
vishṇave prabha-vishṇave || ***(5)*** ||
om namo vishṇave prabha-vishṇave |

My salutations to that Supreme Being Vishnu. By just thinking about Him, all are freed from the bonds of Samsara (liberation about Him, all are freed from the bonds of Samsara (liberation from the cycle of birth, death and rebirth). Salutations to that omnipotent Being!

śrī vaiśampāyana uvācha
śrutvā dharmānaśesheṇa
pāvanāni cha sarvaśaha |
yudhishṭhiraś śāntanavam
punarevābhya bhāshata || ***(6)*** ||

(Note: Shri Vaishampayana was a disciple of Sage Vyasa and is credited to have been the first sage to narrate the Mahabharata to King Janamejeya, the great-grandson of Arjuna. It may be noted that Shri Vaishampayana was only one of the three persons to whom Sage Vyasa had narrated the Mahabharata)

Shri Vaishampayana said: Having heard all the Dharmas in their entirety, Yudhisthira again addressed Bhishma thus:

yudhishṭhira uvācha

kimekam daivatam loke?

kim vāspyekam parāyaṇam?

stuvantah kam? kamarchantaf

prāpnuyurmānavāś śubham? || (7) ||

Yudhisthira asks:

1. Who is the greatest or Supreme God in this World?
2. What is the One Supreme Goal or Refuge that should be sought?

3. By worshipping Whom can man attain auspiciousness (Peace and Prosperity)?

ko dharmas sarva-dharmāṇām
bhavataf paramo mataha? |
kim japanmuchyate jantur
janma samsāra bandhanāt? || (8) ||

4. By worshipping Whom can a Man reach Peace and Prosperity?
5. What, in thy opinion, is the Greatest Dharma?
6. By doing '*japa*' of, what, can creatures go beyond the bonds of *Samsara* (liberation from the cycle of birth, death and rebirth)?

śrī bhīshma uvācha
jagat-prabhum deva-deva
m-anantam purushottamam |
stuvannāma sahasreṇa
purushas satatotthitaha || (9) ||

Shri Bhishma replies:

A person who is engaged in singing and chanting the hymn of the thousand names of Lord Vishnu, the Lord of the Universe, the God of Gods and the limitless Supreme Being!

tameva chārchayannityam

bhaktyā purusha-mavyayam |

dhyāyan stuvannama-syamścha

yajamānastameva cha || (10) ||

And continues to be engaged in worshipping Him who is changeless with devotion, meditating upon Him, glorifying Him, offering obeisance and adoring Him.

anādi nidhanam vishṇum

sarvaloka maheśvaram |

lokādhyaksham stuvannityam

sarva duhkhātigo bhavet || (11) ||

The One who is ever engaged in praising the Lord, who is without a beginning nor end, the ruler of the Universe, the supervisor of the World, the One who is known from the Vedas, the One who is always engaged in the welfare of the Universe, Lord of the Universe and the cause of all Beings, the One who is always engaged in the worship of the Supreme Being, such a One will be freed from all sorrows and pains of this material World.

bramhaṇyam sarva dharmagñam
lokānām kīrti vardhanam |
lokanātham mahadbhūtam
sarvabhūta bhavodbhavam|| (12) ||

He is the champion of all devotees, conversant with all duties and injunctions, the enhancer of fame and achievement of all people, the Master of the Universe, and the Cause of the origin of all Beings.

esha me sarva dharmāṇām
***dharmo*sdhika tamomataha |**
yadbhaktyā puṇḍarīkāksham
stavairarchennaras sadā | (13) ||

The worship of the Supreme Lotus-eyed Lord at all times by a person endowed with devotion is regarded by me as the greatest of all religious practices.

paramam yo mahattejaf
paramam yo mahattapaha |
paramam yo mahad-bramha
paramam yaf parāyaṇam || (14) ||

He, who is the Supreme Effulgence of both Light and Knowledge, He Who is the Ultimate *Tapaswi* or Meditator, He who is the Supreme source of all Knowledge or Brahman, and Who remains the Ultimate Refuge for everyone.

pavitrāṇām pavitram yo
mangaḷānām cha mangaḷam |
daivatam devatānām cha
bhūtānām yo'vyayaḥ pitā || (15) ||

He who is the purest of the Pure, the most auspicious of the auspicious, the God of Gods and the indestructible Progenitor of all Beings.

yatas sarvāṇi bhūtāni
bhavantyādi yugāgame |
yasmimścha pralayam yānti
punareva yugakshaye || (16) ||

From Whom, all Beings originate at the beginning of the First *Yuga,* and in Whom, they merge again at the end of the *Yuga*.

tasya loka pradhānasya
jagannāthasya bhūpate |
vishṇornāma sahasram me
śruṇu pāpa bhayāpaham || (17) ||

O King, hear from me the Thousand Names that removes Sins and drives away fear; the appellations of Vishnu, Lord of the Universe and Ruler of the World.

yāni nāmāni gauṇāni
vikhyātāni mahātmanaha |
ṛshibhif parigītāni
tāni vakshyāmi bhūtaye || (18) ||

For the good of the World, I shall tell you the holy names of the Supreme Being, which are indicative of his attributes and Glory, well-known and recited by the Rishis.

ṛshirnāmnām sahasrasya
***vedavyāso mahāmunihi* ||**
chhandoऽnushṭup tathā devo
***bhagavān devakīsutaha* || *(19)* ||**

The Great Veda Vyasa is the Seer of these Thousand Names of Vishnu; the metre in which it is sung is the Anushtup, and the Presiding Deity is Lord Krishna, the son of Devaki.

amṛtām śūdbhavo bījam
***śaktirdevakinandanaha* |**
trisāmā hṛdayam tasya
***śāntyarthe viniyujyate* || *(20)* ||**

The seed is He-Who-Was born in the Lunar race; its Power is the name of the son of Devaki. The heart is the one who is lauded by the three Sama-hymns, and the purpose of its use is the attainment of Peace.

vishṇum jishṇum mahāvishṇum
prabhavishṇum maheśvaram ||
anekarūpa daityāntam
namāmi purushottamam || (21) ||

I pay my Obeisance to Vishnu, the Victorious, the All-Pervading One, the Mighty Lord of All, the One who took many forms to destroy the Demons (Daityas) and is the Best among all Persons!

Chapter - 2

Pūrvanyāsaha

(Setting the tone)

Any activity requires a certain preliminary build-up or preparation. An athlete does some warm-up before getting on to his/her main event. It is important to create and generate the necessary atmosphere which is conducive to the core activity. In the world of cricket, when a batter is batting well, commentators often remark about the batter being in the 'zone'. In the case of devotion, too, there has to be an enabling build-up. One of the eminent scholars[1] terms this as 'Installation of the Lord'. This 'Installation Ceremony', he says, declares to the devotees that

[1] Swami Chinmayananda in his book 'Thousand ways to the transcendental'

the 'enchanting form of Vishnu' has to be realised as the 'One Infinite Reality' above and beyond all the various forms and avatars that the Lord assumes. When we go to any temple, the presence of the deities, the wafting aroma of the incense, the pujas on offer, and the presence of the devotees all create an atmosphere of devotion or '*bhakti*'. Likewise, the following verses of the '*Pūrvanyāsaha*' set the stage for the chanting of the 'Vishnu Sahasranama':

asya śrī vishṇordivya
sahasranāma stotra mahāmantrasya ||
śrī vedavyāso bhagavān ṛshihi |
anushṭup chandaha |
śrīmahāvishṇuf paramātmā
śrīmannārāyaṇo devatā |.... (a)

amṛtāmśūdbhavo bhānuriti bījam |
devakīnandanas srashṭeti śaktihi |
udbhavaha kshobhaṇo
deva iti paramomantraha |

śankhabhṛnnandakī chakrīti kīlakam |….(b)

śārngadhanvā gadādhara ityastram |
rathāngapāṇi rakshobhya iti netram |
trisāmāsāmagas sāmeti kavacham |
ānandam parabramheti yonihi | …(c)

ṛtussudarśanah kāla iti digbandhaha ||
śrīviśvarūpa iti dhyānam |
śrī mahāvishṇu prītyarthe sahasranāma jape viniyogaha |...(d) (1)

For this '*Maha Mantra*' or sacred chant, viz. The 'Thousand Names of Lord Vishnu', Shri Veda Vyasa is the divine Rishi. Anushtup is the name of the particular Metre in which this sacred chant of Shri Vishnu is sung. Lord Vishnu, who has multiple forms and a variety of names, is the deity of the Chant. Vishnu is the theme of the Chant… (a)

Every deity is a manifestation of the Omnipotence of the Supreme. The creator and sustainer of *Dharma*, the son of Devaki, is the manifested Power of the Almighty. The Creative power invoked and established in the Navel region cannot be conceived by the Mind as such. Therefore, to understand it better, this Mantra conceived the Power as the Lord, who bears the Conch, the Sword and the Discus… (b)

When the Body becomes the temple of the Almighty, it has to be protected like a sacred Treasure House. When Lord Vishnu, the charioteer, is Himself installed in the eyes, the individual is safe in his spiritual Pilgrimage. He Who is glorified by the three types of Samas and whose Glory is itself the manifested Sama Veda. This great Lord is installed as an Armour to wear for self-protection. The Supreme Brahman, the infinite Bliss, is the very Womb from which the Universe has emerged… (c)

Truth, the Lord and his weapon, *Sudarshana*, and His annihilating Power, '*Kala*' or Time, are the mighty forces that guard this sacred temple. The cosmic form of the Lord is the total Universe. Thus, to meditate upon Him as the whole Universe, one has to engage himself in the '*japa*' of the 'Thousand Names of the Lord' for the Grace of Shri Maha Vishnu… (d)

Dhyānam

Kshīro-danvat-pradeśe śuchimaṇi
vilasat saikate mauktikānām
mālāklup-tāsanasthas sphaṭika maṇi
nibhair mauktikair maṇḍi-tāngaha |….(a)

śubhrai rabhrai radabhrai rupari
virachitair muktapīyūsha varshaihi
ānandī naf punīyā darinalina gadā
śankhapāṇir mukundaha ||…..(b)

bhūf pādau yasya nābhir-viyadasura
nilaśchandra sūryau cha netre
karṇāvāśāś śirodyaur-mukhamapi
dahano yasya vāsteyamabdhihi |....(c)

antahstham yasya viśvam sura nara
khagago bhogi gandharva daityaihi
chitram ram ramyate tam tribhuvana
vapuśam vishṇumīśam namāmi ||....(d) (2)

om namo bhagavate vāsudevāya!

Mukunda, who is seated majestically on the banks of the Milky Ocean with the surface sand sparkling like diamonds, is adorning the garland of lustrous pearls… (a)

A Prayer: He, who is in a state of joyous and ecstatic bliss with pure white clouds hovering above, raining showers of nectar, may Mukunda who is holding the discus (*Sudarshana chakra*), the Mace (*Kaumodhaki Gadha*) the conch (*Panchajanya Sankha*), and the Lotus (*Padma*) in His hands purify and liberate us!!... (b)

(Note: There are stories associated with each of the above. The **Sudarshana Chakra**, the story goes, was a weapon given to Lord Krishna by

Lord Shiva to protect the devas from the asuras. The Chakra symbolises the eternal aspect of Time and also the destruction of evil).

Kaumodaki Gada: The word Kaumodaki is derived from the word 'Kumuda', meaning water lily, while the mace represents knowledge, time and intellect. There was a fierce demon by the name of Gada. He had wreaked terror everywhere. Although he was a vicious demon, he was also known to be charitable. Lord Vishnu, disguised as a brahmana, approached the demon to get some bones from his body. Without any hesitation, the demon ripped himself apart and gave bones from his own body to Lord Vishnu, who then created a mace from these bones. He named the mace, Kaumodaki Gada, after the name of the demon himself.

Panchajanya Sankha: Sandipani was the Guru (teacher) of Lord Krishna and his brother Balarama. Guru Sandipani's son had been abducted by a sea demon, Shankasura or Panchajanya, who lived deep inside the Ocean wrapped in a snail's shell. Shankasura had taken Sandipani's son and hidden him inside the shell. It was customary in those days for Gurus to be given a Guru Dakshina from their pupils (an offering in lieu of the teaching imparted by a teacher to his pupils). After their education, Krishna and Balarama wanted their Guru to ask for his Dakshina. The Guru, by way of fees, wanted his son to be rescued and reunited with him. Krishna dived into the Ocean, fought with the demon, vanquished him, brought back the kidnapped son and handed him over to his Guru. Krishna, however, retained the shell with himself, and this came to be known as 'Panchajanya Shankh'. It is believed to produce the primordial sound of Creation which combines in itself the five panchabhutas, viz. Air (Vayu), Water (Jal), Earth (Prithvi), Fire (Agni) and Space (Akasha). The shell also portends the certain destruction of all evil. Krishna had blown his Panchjanya Shankh just before the commencement of the Mahabharata War.

Padma: The Lotus flower or Padma symbolises Lord Vishnu's consort, Lakshmi, and represents water and fertility. According to one of the Puranas, it was from a lotus flower coming out of Lord Vishnu's navel that Lord Brahma, the God of Creation, arose. Lotus also represents Dharma and Purity.

I bow to Lord Vishnu, who has the three worlds as His Body, the Earth as His feet, the Sky as His navel, the Wind as His breath, The Sun and Moon as His eyes, ears as His directions, the Heavens as His head, the Fire as His face, and the Ocean as His abdomen… (c)

In Him is situated the Universe with diverse kinds of *Devas*, men, birds, cattle, serpents, gandharas and *daityas* (demons) - all enjoying a pleasurable life… (d)

śāntākāram bhujagaśayanam

padmanābham sureśam

viśvādhāram gaganasadṛśam

meghavarṇam śubhāngam |

lakshmīkāntam kamalanayanam

yogihṛd dhyānagamyam

vande vishṇum bhavabhayaharam

sarvalokaikanātham || 3 ||

Lord Vishnu, the embodiment of Peace, Calm and Tranquility, reclining on the serpent bed, from Whose navel rises the Lotus Flower (on which Lord Brahma is seated), the God of all Gods, the One who is the cause of the Universe, the One who is as all-pervading as the Sky, the One whose complexion is that of the clouds, the One Whose every part symbolises auspiciousness, the One who is the husband of Goddess Lakshmi, the Lotus-eyed, the One on whom Rishis and Munis meditate, I pay my obeisance to that Lord Vishnu Who dispels fear from the Mind and Who is the Lord of the Universe.

meghaśyāmam pītakauśeyavāsam
śrīvatsānkam kaustubhod bhāsitāngam |
puṇyopetam puṇḍarīkāyatāksham
vishṇum vande sarvalokaika nātham || *4* ||

I salute the Supreme Lord Vishnu, who is dark as the clouds, who is adorned in attractive yellow silk attire, has a SriVatsa mark on his chest, who is radiating with the glow of the Kaustubha gem on his body and is constantly attended to by blessed people.

(**Note**: SriVatsa mark on Lord Vishnu's chest: The Sri in SriVatsa denotes Goddess Lakshmi, the consort of Lord Vishnu who resides in His heart. According to the Bhagavata Purana, a dispute once arose amongst the rishis gathered on the banks of the river Saraswati as to who amongst the three deities of the Trimurti had the greatest patience. It was decided that sage Bhrigu should check this out. Incidentally, sage Bhrigu was the manasaputra (mind-born-son) of Lord Brahma. He was also the author of the most authentic text on predictive astrology (Brighu Samhita). The sage first went to the abode of (his own father) Lord Brahma, Satyaloka. The sage refused to extoll the deity, and Lord Brahma showed his annoyance at this. Lord Shiva in Kailash, too, was found wanting in patience when the sage refused his embrace and instead called him a disruptor of social conventions. This angered Lord Shiva, thus failing in the sage's test of patience. The sage next went to Vaikuntha, the abode of Lord Vishnu. When he found that the deity who was expected to preserve this Universe was sleeping, he got angry and stamped Lord Vishnu on his chest. Lord Vishnu apologised to the sage and told him that he shall forever carry the mark of the stamp by the sage on his chest as a mark of repentance and that this shall also mark the abode of His consort Lakshmi. Since Lord Vishnu did not get provoked and actually treated the sage with great reverence, He rose in the Sage's eyes as the deity with the most patience).

namas samasta bhūtānā
mādi bhūtāya bhūbhṛte |
anekarūpa rūpāya
vishṇave prabhavishṇave || 5 ||

I bow to the Cause of all beings, who upholds and supports the Earth, who comes in various forms (*panchabhutas*, *devas*, humans, *Dashavatara,* etc.). I bow down to that Vishnu, who is the most powerful One.

saśankhachakram sakirīṭakuṇḍalam
sapītavastram sarasīruhekshaṇam |
sahāra vakshas sthala śobhi kaustubham
namāmi vishṇum śirasā chaturbhujam || 6 ||

I pay obeisance to my Lord Vishnu with my head bowed, to the One who is carrying a conch in one hand and a discus in the other, who is wearing a lustrous crown and beautiful earrings and is adorned in yellow silk dress (*vastram*), who has beautiful Lotus-like eyes, who is wearing a necklace on his chest bedecked with the shiny *Kaustubha* Gem and who has four hands.

chhāyāyām pārijātasya
hemasimhāsanopari
āsīnamambudaśyāma
māyatāksha malankṛtam || *7* ||

I take refuge in Lord Krishna - who is seated on a throne made of pure gold under the shade of the Parijata tree, who is dark like a rain-bearing cloud, who has long and beautiful wide eyes, and who is covered with different kinds of adornments (*alankaras)*.

(**Note 1**: **Parijata**: One particular story of the Parijata tree goes thus: Once Sage Narada, while visiting Dwarka, the abode of Lord Krishna, hands over to Him some beautiful flowers from the Parijata tree. Lord Krishna has two consorts - Rukmini and Satyabhama. Krishna hands over the flowers to Rukmini. Sage Narada promptly informs Satyabhama that Krishna has handed over some beautiful flowers to Rukmini. Satyabhama confronts Krishna and demands that the tree which bore these flowers should be planted in her backyard. Krishna then asks Narada where he got these flowers from. Sage Narada says that he got them from Indralok, the abode of Indra. Before Krishna reaches Indralok to get a sapling of the tree, Narada promptly goes and informs Indra that Krishna is on his way to take a sapling of the Parijata tree from his abode. Indra is angry that a sapling is being plucked from his garden without his permission. A fight ensues between Krishna and Indra, and Indra loses, but not before Indra curses that the Parijata tree will henceforth never bear fruits. Krishna returns with the sapling and plants it in a way that while the tree is in the backyard of Satyabhama, all its flowers fall into the backyard of the palace of Rukmini!)

(**Note 2**: Kaustubha gem: As per scriptures the Kaustubha gem is the most radiant gem ever known. It adorns Lord Vishnu's garland and is believed to have come out during the churning of the Ocean (Samudra Manthan).

Kaustubha Gem and Samudra Manthan

chandrānanam chaturbāhum
śrīvatsānkita vakshasam
rukmiṇī satyabhāmābhyām
sahitam kṛshṇamāśraye || 8 ||

My obeisance to the One whose face is beautiful and calm like the Moon, who has four arms, whose chest carries the SriVatsa mark and who is accompanied by His queens Rukmini and Satyabhama.

Chapter - 3

Vishnu Sahasranama

(The Thousand names of Lord Vishnu)

The Creator beyond compare: Before we delve into the shlokas of the Vishnu Sahasranama, let us try to learn a little bit more about the master genius who composed not just these shlokas alone but the entire Mahabharata. The one who created this master epic, made of 100,000 shlokas, covering the multitudinous facets of human behaviour and conduct ranging from greed to generosity, virtuousness to vileness, truth and honesty to deceit and deception, amongst a host of other attributes could only have been a genius well aware of the frailties and strengths of human beings. The Guru Purnima that is celebrated today is a tribute to the birthday of this great saint and scholar.

Veda Vyasa, the creator of these shlokas, is introduced in the Pūrvāngam (The First Part) as the great-grandson of Vashista, the guru of Lord Rama, the grandson of Shakti, the son of Parasara and the father of Suka. The Pūrvāngam even goes to the extent of equating Sage Vyasa to Lord Vishnu:

vyāsāya vishṇu rūpāya
vyāsarūpāya vishṇave |
namo vai bramhanidhaye
vāsishṭhāya namo namaha ||

(My respected salutations to that Vyasa, who is the form of Vishnu and to Vishnu who is a form of Vyasa. My obeisance to Sage Vyasa who is a descendant of Vashishta and who is a treasure house of the knowledge of the *Brahman*).

Vyasa's original name was Krishna Dvaipayana. Those days, people were named almost always with a meaning attached to their names. In this case, 'Krishna' suggested his dark colour or complexion, and 'Dvaipayana' suggested that he was born on an island. Vyasa, a title he acquired later, based on his skills and talent, meant a 'compiler' or 'arranger', which is precisely what this genius had done when he got all the Vedas together and compiled them for easy understanding into four separate and distinct Vedas, viz. Rig Veda, Yajur Veda, Sama Veda and Atharva Veda. Vyasa is also credited with having authored the eighteen Puranas (covering a wide range of topics and legends) and the Brahma Sutras (compilation of Upanishads, which are a part of the Vedas).

What one might ask are the salient features of Vishnu Sahasranama that set it apart from most other shlokas? According to the Vedic scholar, Dushyant Sridhar, there are six salient features of the Vishnu Sahasranama:

1. It encompasses the essence of the great epic Mahabharata;
2. It is something that is revered and acclaimed by the wise *rishis* and *munis*;
3. It was composed by the great and illustrious sage Veda Vyasa, who was also a compiler of the Vedas (the largest

body of ancient texts codifying Vedic rituals and practices containing the essence of philosophy and religion) and *Brahma Sutras* (a Sanskrit text which puts together ideas and practices from the Upanishads);

4. Let us not forget that it was sung by a *Mahajana* and one of the most ardent devotees of Lord Vishnu, Bhishma;

5. It was recognised as a very effective and immensely helpful composition not just by scholars and wise men but even by medical treatises like Charaka Samhita; dramatists, authors and poets like Banabhatta or astrologers like Rishi Parasara; it has been commented upon by acharyas of the three *Mathas* viz. *Advaita* (Adi Shankara), *Vishishta Advaita* (Ramanuja/ Parasara Bhattar) and *Dvaita* philosophies (Madhava);

6. The Vishnu Sahasranama embodies not just the essence of Mahabharata but also that of the Bhagavad Gita.

Lord Vishnu: the *numero uno*: What about the subject of the Vishnu Sahasranama viz. Lord Vishnu himself? One aspect which is more than evident in reading or listening to the Vishnu Sahasranama is the nature of Lord Vishnu himself - a complete package! Lord Vishnu is not just the Creator of this Universe of matter, full of animate and inanimate objects and creatures, but also an integral part of that creation. It would, therefore, be appropriate and correct to say that the Creator of all of us also lives within each one of us. There are several words in the Vishnu Sahasranama (as we will notice in the English translations of the shlokas) which state that Lord Vishnu created the Universe from Himself and that he also absorbed the entire Universe within Himself at the time of deluge, thus making Him the Creator, Controller and Regulator of the Wheel of Life. He is described as omnipotent, omnipresent, omniscient, the Creator, Sustainer, Nourisher and Destroyer of all beings in this Universe; the One who transcends Time, Space and Matter; the One who is neither born nor decays nor dies; the One who is self-created. He is free from attachments, unchangeable, equanimous, and the One who assumes and manifests Himself at different periods in Time as various *Avataras* (*Dashavatara*), graceful, loving (In Shloka 78; *nāma* 736 of the Sahasranama He is described as '*Bhaktavatsalaha*' meaning 'One with unbounded love for His devotees'), a 'friend of the world' ('*Lokabandhu*': shloka 78; *nāma* 733), protective towards his devotees (examples of Prahlada, His young devotee and Draupadi, the wife of the Pandavas), affectionate, merciful, patient (he forgives as many as 100 faults of Sisupala before beheading him with His *Sudarshana Chakra*), lenient to faults of his devotees and yet fierce and unsparing in taking action against the evil-minded (examples of Ravana, the *rakshasa* king of Lanka and Kamsa, His own Uncle). These and many more such attributes have been brought out by Sage Vyasa in the Vishnu Sahasranama.

Although we often hear of *Trimurti,* meaning the triumvirate of Vishnu, Shiva and Brahma, Sage Vyasa himself was absolutely in no doubt as to who the Supreme Lord was. There is a Shloka in the *Phalashruti* (reproduced below) of the Vishnu Sahasranama where Lord Shiva is telling his consort, Goddess Parvati, that he himself keeps chanting Rama's name and that chanting the name of Rama (none other than Lord Vishnu himself) is equivalent to the chanting of the thousand names of Lord Vishnu.

śrīrāma rāma rāmeti
rame rāme manorame |
sahasranāma tattulyam
rāmanāma varānane ||

In Sloka 52 of the Vishnu Sahasranama, Lord Vishnu is spoken of as '*Aadidevo*', meaning the 'First Deity' or the God of all Gods. In Sloka 69, He is referred to as '*Kesavah*'. While on a literal plane, it refers to Krishna (*avatara* of Lord Vishnu) as the One with long hairs, it might also refer to 'the rays that illumine' or '*Kesas*' and the one having this attribute as '*Kesava*' (none other than Lord Vishnu Himself) in which '*Ka*' refers to Brahma the Creator and '*Eesa*' refers to Shiva, the Destroyer. Both these deities are subsumed, therefore, in Vishnu, the Preserver, who goes by the epithet '*Kesavah*'.

In Shloka 104 of the Vishnu Sahasranama, there is the word '*Pra-pitaamahah*' which means 'One who is the father of even the father of all beings', the Creator, Lord Brahma. As per the Puranas, Lord Brahma is himself stated to have arisen from the lotus, which emerged from the navel of Lord Vishnu.

Dashavatara

The Abiding Theme:

If there is one abiding theme of the answers given by Bhisma to Yudhisthira, it is DEVOTION or Bhakti. Bhishma asks Yudhisthira to regularly chant the Vishnu Sahasranama with devotion, sincerity and regularity in order to get rid of all his doubts and confusions and also to attain *Moksha* or liberation from the cycle of birth and rebirth. Bhishma himself demonstrated the intensity of his devotion in full measure by engaging in a conversation with Yudhisthira and narrating the entire Vishnu Sahasranama while ignoring the pain and discomfort of lying on a bed of arrows even while being soaked in blood and mortally wounded.

The celestial sage Narada says that *Bhakti* or devotion to the Lord is above and beyond all other spiritual practices. In Chapter 18 of the Bhagavad Gita, Krishna tells Arjuna that the only way he can realise Him (God) is through *Bhakti* or devotion. He also says that it is from a state of *atmagyan* (self-realisation) that a *gyani* (a scholar) engages in devotion. Interestingly, in the Bhagvatam, Sri Krishna says that although He is supremely independent, the *bhakti* of a devotee makes Him dance much like a snake charmer gets a snake to dance to the swaying of his flute. The Puranas quote Krishna as telling Arjuna, 'I become a slave of those devotees of mine, who chant my names and keep me close to them in their thoughts, this is a fact, Oh Arjuna.' The chanting and listening to the Vishnu Sahasranama is a manifestation of the *Bhakti* being referred to above, and therefore, is it any wonder that the Sahasranama is so widely and popularly chanted and listened to by hundreds and thousands of people all over the world.

A quintessential requirement for devotion is complete surrender (*Pranidhana*) and banishing one's ego (*Ahamkara*). When Draupadi was dragged to the Hastinapura court and was being disrobed by Dushasana, the brother of Duryodhana, the eldest Kaurava Prince, she fervently prayed to Lord Krishna for help after not getting it from any other quarter. It was after a slight time lag that Krishna came to support and protect her from the humiliation. The more Dushasana tried to disrobe her, the more cloth took its place to drape her, and he had to give up on this vile act finally. Krishna had played his invisible role as a Protector and Saviour! Later, when Draupadi questions Krishna as to why he delayed coming to her help, Krishna's reply spelt out the importance He attached to the act of surrender. He told her that He could not come as long as she kept holding on to a small strand of her clothing, and it was possible for Him to come only after she had released that - indicative of her complete surrender!

In the Ramayana, Hanuman emerges as an embodiment of the purest form of devotion to his Lord, Rama. In the Bhagavad Gita, Krishna himself declares that among devotees, he is Prahlada.

Picture of Hanuman seated at the feet of Sri Rama in the presence of Sita and Lakshmana

There is a story about Prahlada in the Puranas. Hiranyakashipu was a demon (*asura*) king. When his wife, Kayadhu, became pregnant, Indra, the King of Gods, thinking that the world could ill afford to bear the scourge of yet another demon, decided to do away with the child in the womb of Kayadhu. However, Narada, the celestial saint, intervened, and took it upon himself to constantly whisper the name of Lord Vishnu into the ears of Kayadhu so that the child growing in the womb would be born of a divine heart, unlike his wicked asura father. This is exactly what happened. The child named Prahlada, meaning the one who brings infinite joy and bliss, became an ardent devotee of Lord Vishnu. Hiranyakashipu was most unhappy with this situation. Haughty and arrogant on the back of the boon he had received from Lord Brahma that he could not be killed by any weapon, nor by any man nor beast, nor during the day nor night, nor on the Earth nor in the skies, and having failed to get young Prahlada killed for uttering the name of Lord Vishnu, he confronted his son and asked him if his Lord was present in the pillar. Prahlada told Hiranyakashipu that Lord Vishnu was everywhere (*Sarvatra*), including the pillar. When Hiranyakashipu angrily pounded on the pillar, it was Narasimha (man with the face of a lion and one of the *avataras* of Lord Vishnu) who burst out of the pillar, took Hiranyakashipu on his lap, and ripped him apart with his huge nails. After this, when Narasimha asked Prahlada to ask for a boon, what he asked for set new standards for *nishkam bhakti* namely, a devotion beyond greed, desire and self. Prahlada simply asked the Lord to make his heart in such a way that he would never ever seek or ask anything for himself from the Lord in the future. It was, therefore, no surprise for the Lord to say that among devotees, he is Prahlada!

Hiranyakashipu

The inspiring story of the devotion of yet another young boy from the Puranas is that of Dhruva. Dhruva's father, King Uttanpad, had two wives and from each of these wives, he had one son. The son from the first wife, Suniti, was Dhruva, while the son from the second wife, Surichi, was Uttam. The King was besotted with Surichi and Uttam. Dhruva and his mother were relegated both in terms of position as well as love and affection. All that Dhruva required was some love from his father. Once when he was not even allowed to sit on the lap of his father, he felt very sad and discriminated against. He went crying to his mother, Suniti who told him that the only one who could address his sorrows was Lord Narayana. The boy, determined to find a solution to his woes, went into the nearby forest of Madhuvan on the banks of the River Yamuna, where he met the celestial sage Narada. The Sage gave the boy a mantra and asked him to chant this relentlessly to invoke the Lord. Dhruva was so sincere and intense in his invoking of Lord Vishnu that He finally appeared before him bowled over by the boy's single-minded devotion. He blessed Dhruva and asked him to go back and rule the kingdom, which was rightfully his. After his time on the Earth, he was promised an abode higher than that of the other gods (*devas*) and *rishis*. Not just that! The Lord was so pleased with him that He also blessed him with a life span much more than that of the *devas* themselves. Dhruva continues to adorn the skies as '*Dhruva Tara*' or the Pole Star – serving as an abiding reminder and testimony to the devotion of a young and brave boy towards Lord Vishnu.

Lord Vishnu appearing in front of Dhruva

Bhakti has always been an abiding theme in India from ancient times. The '*Navadha Bhakti*' (nine ways to express or develop devotion for God), first expressed by Prahlada, was sung by medieval saints like Chaitanya Mahaprabhu. In medieval India, the Bhakti cult was propounded by saints and devotees, starting from the Vaishnava Alvars and Shaiva Nayanars to the likes of Ramanuja, Madhavacharya, Saint Tukaram, Ramdas, Sant Kabir, Shri Guru Nanak Dev, Mira bai and many others who had a huge impact and following in the contemporary India of then.

There are several shlokas and words in the Vishnu Sahasranama where the states of consciousness have been mentioned. These states have been variously described in the Sahasranama as 'three cities' or 'three worlds' which refers basically to the states of wakefulness, dreams and deep sleep. Above and beyond these three states is the state of Pure Consciousness or *Turiya* (also known as *Chaturiya* or *Chaturtha,* denoting the fourth state), where the Self or Infinite Reality is realised.

Let us now move on to the *shlokas* (translations have been done for the shloka as a whole rather than taking it word by word, which would make it copious) composed by the master 'craftsman', Veda Vyasa, and as sung by the great Bhishma where life has been infused into every single word, embellished with metaphors making the readers marvel at the sheer genius and creativity of this most abiding and popular work doused in pure devotion:

(Each Shloka will need to be read with its corresponding translated meaning more than once to be able to understand better and relate to it)

Vishnu Sahasranama

viśvam vishṇur vashaṭkāro
bhūtabhavyabhavatprabhuhu|
bhūtakṛd bhūtabhṛd bhāvo
bhūtātmā bhūtabhāvanaha || 1 ||

The One who pervades everything; the One who is propitiated; the One who is the Lord of the Past, Future and Present (transcending the frontiers of Time); the One who is the Creator, Destroyer and Sustainer of the Universe; the One who is the nourisher of all creatures; the One who exists in everything - living and non-living; the One who is the Soul or *Atma* of everything, the One who is responsible for the birth and growth of all creatures.

pūtātmā paramātmā cha
muktānām paramāgatihi |
avyayaf purushas sākshī
kshetragño'kshara eva cha || 2 ||

The One who is pure; the One who is the Supreme Reality; the One who is the Final Destination and thoughts of Whom will ensure *Moksha* or liberation from the cycle of births and rebirths; the One who is indestructible, has no decay and is Eternal; the One who resides in the Body and sees everything but yet remains unaffected by anything; the One who knows the

Body and all that goes within it; the One who remains Infinite and Eternal.

yogo yogavidām netā
pradhāna purusheśvaraha |
nārasimhavapuś śrīmān
keśavaf purushottamaha || 3 ||

The One who can be attained by Yoga; the One who takes care of all those who are seeking and devoted to Him; The One who is a master of those established in Yoga; The One who is the Infinite Reality; the One whose form is half human and half lion (the reference is to 'Narasimha', avatara of Lord Vishnu,and Who using this form, destroyed the tyrant, Hiranyakashipu, and blessed his devotee, Prahlada); the One who is always with Sree meaning Mother Lakshmi; the One who is beautiful and graceful with locks of hair ('*kesa*'); and the One who is best among all the imperishable Souls or Self or Infinite Reality.

sarvaś śarvaś śivas
sthāṇur bhūtādir nidhiravyayaha |
sambhavo bhāvano bhartā
prabhavaf prabhurīśvaraha || 4 ||

He who is the Beginning and the end of All; He who is the auspicious One; He who is eternally pure; the One who is permanent; the One who is the cause of the five elements or the '*Pancha Bhootas*' (Space, Air, Water, Fire and Earth); the One who is the imperishable and unchangeable Treasure; the One who manifests Himself in different forms; the One who gives freely and generously to His devotees; the One who governs the entire living world; the One from whom the five elements originate; the Lord who is all powerful; the One who is Supreme.

svayambhūś śambhurādityaf
pushkarāksho mahāsvanaha |
anādinidhano dhātā
vidhātā dhāturuttamaha || 5 ||

He who manifests on His own; He who bestows happiness on his devotees; He who is the golden splendour in the sun's orb; He who has Lotus-like eyes; He who has a thundering voice; The One who has neither birth nor death nor change; The One who is behind all forms; The One who is dispenser of all, "fruits of actions"; The One who is The Supreme Controller of the Universe; The One from Whom all elements, creatures, and Forms have originated.

aprameyo hṛshīkeśaf

padmanābhoऽmaraprabhuhu|

viśvakarmā manustvashṭā

sthavishṭhas sthaviro dhruvaha || 6 ||

The One who cannot be measured, defined nor realised by the five senses; The One who provides light to the sense organs; The One from whose navel springs a Lotus flower bearing the four-faced creator Brahma; The Lord of the Devas; The One who created all objects and experiences; The One who has manifested Himself in the Vedic Mantras; The One who can subsume in Himself the entire Universe; The One who is not impacted by Time and who is changeless.

agrāhyaś śāśvatah kṛshṇo
lohitākshaf pratardanaha |
prabhūtas trikakubdhāma
pavitram mangalam param || 7 ||

The One who cannot be perceived or understood; The One who is permanent and changeless; The One who removes the sins from the hearts of those who meditate upon Him; The One who is Red- Lotus eyed; The One who is the destroyer of the Universe at the Time of the Great Dissolution (*Pralaya*); The One who is ever full and perfect; The One who supports the three realms of consciousness namely, the state of wakefulness, state of dreams, and state of deep sleep; The One who bestows purity in the heart of those who meditate upon Him; The One who brings joy and consciousness into the hearts of his devotees.

īśānaf prāṇadaf prāṇo
jyeshṭhaś śreshṭhaf prajāpatihi
hiraṇyagarbho bhūgarbho
mādhavo madhusūdanaha || 8 ||

The Controller of the five great elements; The One who is the Giver of Life; The One who is immortal and eternal; The One who is the oldest and also infinite; The One who is most qualified or praiseworthy; The One who is the Father, or Creator of all creatures; The One who dwells in the womb of the world; The One from whom the world has emerged; The One who is the spouse of Mahalakshmi; The One who is sought by a devotee who has stilled his mind; The One who destroyed the demon Madhoo, and The One who is meditated upon as the Supreme Reality.

īśvaro vikramī dhanvī
medhāvī vikramah kramaha |
anuttamo durādharshah
kṛtagñah kṛtirātmavān || 9 ||

The One who is omnipotent; The One who is full of prowess and courage; The One who is the wielder of the bow, Saarnga; The One who is supremely intelligent; The One who travels around the world on the white eagle, Garuda; The One who helps in crossing *samsara* (the cycle of birth, death and rebirth); The One who is great and beyond comparison; The One who cannot be attacked or defeated; The One who knows the activities of everyone; The One who rewards the good and punishes the evil; The One who dwells in all of us and is omnipotent.

sureśaś śaraṇam śarma
viśvaretāf prajābhavaha |
ahas samvatsaro vyālaf
pratyayas sarvadarśanaha || 10 ||

The One who is the God of Gods; The One who is the ultimate destination for all his devotees; The One who is Infinite Bliss; The One from whom the Tree of Life has arisen; The One who is Time itself; The One who is difficult to grasp by those who have no devotion; The One who is

Supreme Knowledge; The One who is omnipresent and omniscient.

ajas sarveśvaras siddhas
siddhis sarvādirachyutaha |
vṛshākapirameyātmā
sarvayoga vinissṛtaha || 11 ||

The One who was never born; The Lord of everything; The One who has nothing more to achieve; The One who can bestow *moksha* meaning liberation from the cycle of birth and rebirth; The One who is the very beginning of All; The One who is the Supreme Reality; The One who lifts the world from the sunken depths of *adharma* or unrighteousness to the beautiful heights of *Dharma* or righteousness; The One who can manifest Himself in any form; The One who is beyond all *Yogas* or contacts or attachments.

vasur vasumanās satyas
samātmā sammitas samaha |
amoghaf puṇḍarīkāksho
vṛshakarmā vṛshākṛtihi || 12 ||

The One who supports all elements; The One who has a mind which is Supremely Pure and free from all likes and dislikes; The One who remains constant; The One who is present equally in everyone; The One who has been accepted by the *Rishis* and the Upanishads as the 'One Truth' and 'Infinite Reality'; The One who can be contacted and experienced; The One who always acts to establish *Dharma* and who assures to be there in every age to uphold and establish *Dharma.*

rudro bahuśirā babhrur
viśvayoniś śuchiśravāha |
amṛtaś śāśvatasthāṇur
varāroho mahātapāha || 13 ||

The One who removes all sorrows for his devotees; The One who has many heads, thousand eyes, ears, hands, and feet; The One who rules over the worlds; The One from whom both thoughts and actions have arisen; The One with beautiful and efficient ears; The One who is immortal and immutable; The One who is permanent and irremovable; The One who is the ultimate destination for self-realization; The One who is the embodiment of knowledge and consciousness.

sarvagas sarva vidbhānur
vishvakseno janārdanaha |
vedo vedavida-vyango
vedāngo vedavitkavihi || 14 ||

The One who pervades everything; The One who is the all-knowing Effulgent Consciousness; The One facing whom even the army of the gods retreats and scatters; The One who gives sorrow and joy to the wicked and good people, respectively; The One who is all knowing; The One who knows the Vedas; The One who is devoid of any imperfections; The One whose limbs are the Vedas; The One who reflects upon the Vedas; The One who is wise and experienced.

lokādhyakshas surādhyaksho
dharmādhyakshah kṛtākṛtaha |
chaturātmā chatur-vyūhaś
chaturdamshṭraś chaturbhujaha || ***15*** ||

The One who is the Lord of the worlds; The One who is the Lord of the *devas* or Gods; The One who guides us in following and observing *dharma*; The One from whom everything manifests and also The One from whom nothing manifests; The One who has four manifestations or *Vibhooties* which are reflected in His roles as Creator, Sustainer, Destroyer and the Self or *Atma-Vibhooti*; The One who has four mighty powers (*vyuhas*) for the purpose of creation namely, Vasudeva, Samkarshana, Pradyumna, and Aniruddha; The One who took the form of Narasimha to protect Prahlada; The One who has four hands carrying the *Shankh* (conch), *Padma* (lotus), *Chakra* (discus) and *Gada* (mace).

bhrājishṇur-bhojanam bhoktā
***sahishṇur-jagadādijaha* |**
anagho vijayo jetā
***viśvayonif punarvasuhu* || *16* ||**

The effulgent One, who illumines everything, including the sun, moon, and the stars. He is an object of enjoyment as well as an enjoyer. He forgives us for our faults and helps us by conquering avoidable thoughts and actions. He is the One who was there at the very beginning, and he is also there at the time of the dissolution of the Universe. He is not tainted or contaminated by anything. He is sinless. He is ever victorious, for he is the One infinite reality that triumphs over all manifestations of matter. He is the source or cause of everything in the Universe. He is the "Self" in all objects of his creation.

upendro vāmanaf prāmśu
ramoghaś śuchirūrjitaha |
atīndras sangrahas sargo
dhṛtātmā niyamo yamaha || 17 ||

The One who is the younger brother of Indra (In the '*Vamana*' avatara of Lord Vishnu, he was born to Aditi, the mother of Indra); The One who took the form of a "*Vamana*" (one having a small body); the One who is very tall (gigantic) (and in the three steps that he sought from Mahabali, the kind, generous but proud asura king, he covered all the three worlds and that included conquering Mahabali and his pride); the One who does nothing without a great purpose; the One who is ever pure and is also a bestower of purity on his devotees; The One who is the fountain head of strength; The One who transcends the mind; The One who holds everything together at the time of the deluge; The One who is the creator of the Universe and also has the Universe within him. The controller and enforcer of all forces and laws of nature.

vedyo vaidyas sadāyogī
vīrahā mādhavo madhuhu |
atīndriyo mahāmāyo
mahotsāho mahābalaha || 18 ||

The One goal after knowing which everything else gets known; The One who is the master of all knowledge; The One who seeks His identity in the Self; The One who destroys the Asuras conceited and drunk by Power and Tyranny; The One who is the Lord of knowledge; The One who instils joy, happiness, and bliss like nectar in the hearts of his devotees; The One who is beyond sense organs; The One who is Supreme Consciousness; The One who is the Supreme Accomplisher; The One who is omnipotent.

mahābuddhir-mahāvīryo
mahāśaktir-mahādyutihi |
anir-deśyavapuś śrīmā
nameyātmā mahādridhṛk || 19 ||

The One who is omniscient; The One who is full of vigour, energy and radiance; The One who is all powerful; The One who is Effulgent; The One who cannot be described; The One who is glorious, The One who cannot be measured; The One who supports the great mountains (the reference here is to two instances: one in which the Lord assumed the form of *Koorma* (The Great Tortoise) in order to support the Mandara mountain during the churning process of the milky ocean and the other when he lifted the Govardhana mountain in order to protect the cows and people of Vrindavan).

maheshvāso mahībhartā

śrīnivāsas satāngatihi |

aniruddhas surānando

govindo govidām patihi || 20 ||

The One who wields the bow *Śāranga*; The One who supports the Earth; The One in whom Lakshmi, the Goddess of wealth, resides; The One who is the final goal for all spiritual seekers; The One who cannot be stopped; The causer of happiness; The One who is the protector of cows, *Vedas*, speech and the Earth; The One who is the Lord of all those who are men of wisdom.

marīchir-damano hamsas
suparṇo bhujagottamaha |
hiraṇyanābhas sutapāf
padmanābhaf prajāpatihi ||21||

The One who is the embodiment of illumination; The One who exercises control and restraint on all negativities in one's heart; The One who is self-realised; The One who is like the bird with beautiful wings who sits still and observes; The One who is Ananta, the best among the serpents; The One who supports the creation from his navel; The One who has supreme control over his sense organs; The One who has lotus which springs out of his navel; The One who is the Lord of all beings, since every creature has emerged from Him - In other words, the Lord is the (*Pati*) Father of all living creatures (*Prajaa*).

amṛtyus sarvadṛk simhas
sandhātā sandhimām-sthiraha |
ajo durmarshaṇaś śāstā
viśrutātmā surārihā || 22 ||

The One who is changeless and not subject to birth, growth, decay, disease and death; The One who knows and sees everything; The One with the powers of destruction and change; The One who is a regulator of the 'fruits of action'; The One who is conditioned by His own actions as well as the results of those actions; The One who is ever firm, stable and consistent; The One who is without birth; The One who is invincible; The One who is the ruler of the Universe; The One who is very well known; The One who destroys the enemies of the *suras* (Gods).

gurur-gurutamo dhāma
satyas satyaparākramaha |
nimishoऽnimishas sragvī
vāchaspati-rudāradhīhi ||23||

The One who is both the author and teacher of the Vedas; The One who is the destination for all devotees; The One who is the Absolute Truth; The One who is of great valour; The One who, with his eyes closed, is in deep contemplation but nevertheless always awake; The One with unblinking eyes; The One who is always wearing the garland of non-decaying flowers; The Lord whose mind encompasses everything and who is tolerant of a devotee's fault.

agraṇīr grāmaṇīś śrīmān
nyāyo netā samīraṇaha
sahasramūrdhā viśvātmā
sahasrākshas sahasrapāt||24||

The One who leads us to the peak; The One who controls, guides and leads the collections of many things; One who is most effulgent; The One who can decide and assess on the basis of reasoning and logic; The One who is a leader; The One who in the form of breath controls all motion; The One with a thousand heads; The One who is the essence of all living creatures;

The One with a thousand eyes; The One with a thousand feet.

āvartano nivṛttātmā

samvṛtas sampramardanaha |

ahas samvartako vanhi

ranilo dharaṇīdharaha || 25 ||

The causer of the cycle of birth and death; The One who is the Pure Self; The One who is completely immersed; The One who causes destruction of the evil-minded; The One who causes the movements or change of days; The One who carries the offerings of a *yagna*; The One who is in eternal movement; The One who supports the Earth.

suprasādaf prasannātmā

viśvadhṛg-viśvabhug-vibhuhu |

satkartā satkṛtas sādhur

janhur-nārāyaṇo naraha || 26 ||

The One who is liberal in bestowing his grace even on those, who are not kind to Him; The One who is ever pleasant and blissful; The source of all existence; The One who enjoys all experiences; The One who manifests himself in different forms; The One who is very welcoming to those who are good and virtuous; The One who is worshipped by all living creatures; The One who always treads the righteous path; The One who leads all creatures along the path of the cosmic law; The One who is the abode of all beings; The One who guides all creatures.

asankhyeyo'sprameyātmā
viśishṭaś śishṭakṛch chhuchihi |
siddhārthas siddhasankalpas
siddhidas siddhi sādhanaha|| 27 ||

The One with innumerable names and forms; The One who cannot be known or measured; The One whose glory is supreme; The One who governs everything; The One who is pure; The One for whom there is nothing more to be gained or achieved; The One whose all wishes are fulfilled; The One who is the giver of rewards for those involved in spiritual practices; The One who is the enabler of attainment and fulfilment.

vṛshāhī vṛshabho vishṇur

vṛshaparvā vṛshodaraha |

vardhano vardhamānaścha

viviktaś śrutisāgaraha ||28||

The One who is the controller of all actions and dispenser of results; The One who showers blessings on His devotees; The One who is all-pervading; The One who leads to eternal *Dharma*; The One from whose belly all beings are born; The One who is the nurturer and nourisher of life; The One who can grow and assume any size and form; The One who is distinct and separate from everything; The One from whom all the Vedas and knowledge flows just like rivers flow into an Ocean.

subhujo durdharo vāgmī

mahendro vasudo vasuhu |

naikarūpo bṛhadrūpaś

śipivishṭaf prakāśanaha || 29 ||

The One with graceful arms; The One who cannot be understood even by great Yogis; The One who encompasses all glories of the Universe; The One who is the Lord of Gods; The One who grants wealth and prosperity externally and inner well-being internally; The One who signifies prosperity; The One who has infinite forms; The One who is vast and gigantic; The One who resides in the rays of the Sun; The One who lights up or illuminates everything.

ojastejodyutidharaf
prakāśātmā pratāpanaha |
ṛddhas spashṭāksharo mantraś
chandrāmśur bhāskaradyutihi || 30 ||

The One who possesses good health (*Ojas*); The One who has gathered certain brilliance because of his way of life (*Tejas*) and because of these two qualities develops an aura (*Dyuti)* of divinity; The One who embodies brightness; The One who causes glow; The One who is full of prosperity; the vehicle through which we can experience the Lord; The One who is an embodiment of the moon; The One who is endowed with the effulgence of the Sun.

amṛtāmśūdbhavo bhānuś
śaśabindus sureśvaraha |
aushadham jagatas setus
satyadharmaparākramaha || 31||

The One who is a nourisher; The One who is self-effulgent; The one who is the rabbit-shaped spot on the moon; The One who is a Lord of all the *suras* or Gods; The One who is a divine medicine; The One who is a bridge that can help cross all the obstacles and frailties to reach Supreme Reality: The One who always stands and fights for truth and righteousness.

bhūtabhavyabhavannāthaf
pavanaf pāvanosnalaha |
kāmahā kāmakṛt kāntah
kāmah kāmapradaf prabhuhu || 32 ||

The One who is the Lord of the past, present and future; The One who is the life-sustaining atmosphere; The One who exemplifies the breeze that purifies the atmosphere; The One who is the embodiment of fire; The One who destroys desires; The One who fulfils all desires; The One who is enchanting; The One who is sought by all creatures; The One who fructifies all desires; The One who is the Supreme Master.

yugādi kṛdyugāvarto
naikamāyo mahāśanaha |
adṛśyo vyaktarūpaścha
sahasrajida -nantajit || ***33*** ||

The One who is the cause of the four *yugas*; The One who causes the change of the *yugas* (*Satya, Tretaa, Dvaapara and Kali*); The One who has many manifestations; The One who consumes everything; The One who is not perceived by the sense organs; The One who has a clear form; The One who has vanquished thousands of demons or *Rakshasas* (philosophically, it refers to lower impulses like greed, jealousy, etc.); The One who is ever victorious in attaining Higher Consciousness.

ishṭoऽviśishṭaś śishṭeshṭaś

śikhaṇḍī nahusho vṛshaha |

krodhahā krodhakṛtkartā

viśvabāhur mahīdharaha || 34

The One who is loved by all; The One who presides over every single activity in all creatures; The One who is dearest to all his seekers; The One who has a peacock feather; The One who binds all; The One who is the fulfiller of all desires; The One who destroys anger; The One who helps his devotees to control the baser instincts; The One who has many hands to do a variety of activities in the Universe; The One who supports the Earth or One who receives all forms of worship.

achyutaf prathitaf prāṇaf

prāṇado vāsavānujaha |

apām nidhi-radhishṭhāna

mapramattaf pratishṭhitaha || 35 ||

The One who is steady and constant; The One who is all-pervading; The One who is a manifestation of life in all creatures; The granter of life; The One born as a younger brother of Indra; The Treasure of all waters, viz the ocean; The One who is a foundation of the Universe; The One who can never be deluded or the One who never makes a wrong judgment; The One who is the Ultimate Cause.

skandas skandadharo

dhuryo varado vāyuvāhanaha |

vāsudevo bṛhad-bhānu

rādidevaf purandaraha || ***36*** ||

The One whose glory is expressed through Subramanya, the son of Lord Shiva; The One who upholds righteousness; The One who continuously carries out the process of creation, sustenance and annihilation; the granter of boons to his devotees; The One who causes the movement of the winds; The One who both dwells and supports all things in the Universe; The One who possesses great illumination; The

One who is the foremost amongst the *devas*; the One who is a destroyer of the three 'cities' namely, waking, dreams and deep sleep.

aśoka-stāraṇa-stāraś
śūraś śaurir-janeśvaraha |
anukūlaś śatāvartaf
padmī padmanibhekshaṇaha || 37 ||

The One without sorrows, The One who enables us to cross the different stages to self-realisation and liberation from the cycle of births and deaths; The One who is a saviour; The One who is valiant; The One who has been born into the family of Soora (Soorasena being the father of Vasudeva, the father of Krishna); The Lord of all creatures; The One who is a friend of everyone; The One who manifests himself in many forms; The One with the Lotus in his hand; The One whose eyes are as beautiful as the Lotus.

padmanābhoꞩravindākshaf

padmagarbhaś śarīrabhṛt |

mahardhir-ṛddho vṛddhātmā

mahāksho garuḍadhvajaha || ***38*** ||

One who has the Lotus in his navel; The One who has eyes as beautiful as the Lotus, The One who is meditated upon in the centre of the lotus-of-the heart; The sustainer and nourisher of the body; The One who has great prosperity and power; The One who has expanded himself in all realms; The "Self" from whom the world of plurality has emerged; The One who has great eyes and misses nothing, meaning the Consciousness which illumines everything at all times in all bosoms; The One with Garuda, the eagle, on His flag.

atulaś śarabho bhīmas

samayagño havirharihi |

sarvalakshaṇalakshaṇyo

lakshmīvān samitiñjayaha || ***39*** ||

The One who is incomparable; The One who resides and shines through the bodies; The One who is fierce; The One who is equanimous all times; The receiver of oblations; The One who is Himself the proof regardless of the method of enquiry; The One who is the consort of Lakshmi; The One who is ever victorious.

viksharo rohito mārgo
hetur-dāmodaras sahaha |
mahīdharo mahābhāgo
vegavā-namitāśanaha || 40 ||

The One who is imperishable; The One who is incarnated in the form of a fish (*Matsya avatara*); The One who is both the way and the destination; The One who is the cause for the creation of the Universe; The One whose mind stands purified by self-control; The all enduring One; The supporter or the bearer of the Earth; The One who has beautiful limbs; The One who has enormous speed; The One who has an "endless appetite" meaning the Higher Consciousness consuming all the other three states, namely, waking, dreaming and deep sleep.

udbhavaha kshobhaṇo devas
śrīgarbhaf parameśvaraha |
karaṇam kāraṇam kartā
vikartā gahano guhaha || 41 ||

The One who is the source of creation; The One who is the cause of destruction; The One who shines as the Universal Consciousness; The One who contains all Glories within oneself; The One who is the Supreme Ruler; The One who is the instrument of creation; The One who is the cause of creation; The performer of the functions of creation, sustenance and destruction; The One who has created from Himself his many forms; The One who cannot be understood by the known instruments of knowledge; The One who is the very core of every living creature.

vyavasāyo vyavasthānas
samsthānas sthānado dhruvaha
parardhif paramaspashṭas
***tushṭaf pushṭaś śubhekshaṇaha* || *42* ||**

The One with a focused mind; The One who controls and regulates the Laws of the Universe; The One who absorbs within himself everyone and everything during the time of the deluge; The One who disperses the fruits of action; The One who is steadfast and fixed; The One who has many manifestations; The One with extreme clarity; The One who is always happy and pleased with whatever is offered to Him even if that be little; The One who is ever-full; The One with the auspicious gaze.

rāmo virāmo virato
***mārgoneyo nayoऽnayaha* |**
vīraś śaktimatām śreshṭho
***dharmo dharmaviduttamaha* || *43* ||**

The One who is the Supreme Consciousncss sought by *Yogis* and *Rishis*; The One who is the abode of all creatures; The One unaffected by the agitations of the mind; The One path to attain him; The One who guides and shows his devotees the way to Reality; The One who leads; The One who leads all but is not led by any; The One who is valiant; The best amongst the powerful; The One who regulates and controls the Cosmic Law of sustainability; The foremost amongst those who have realised *Dharma*.

vaikuṇṭhaf purushaf prāṇaf
prāṇadaf praṇavaf pṛthuhu |
hiraṇyagarbhaś śatrughno
vyāpto vāyu-radhokshajaha || ***44*** ||

The One who wards off men from wrong-doings; The One who dwells in all bodies; The Life force that exists in the body; The One who bestows life; The cosmic sound Om; The One who is all pervasive; The life-giving Power of Air; The One whose senses are directed inwards.

ṛtus sudarśanah kālaf
parameshṭhī parigrahaha |
ugras samvatsaro daksho
viśrāmo viśvadakshiṇaha || 45 ||

The One who is the Lord of the seasons; The One who is easy to seek with devotion; The One who is the personification of Space and Time; The One who is centred in His own infinite Glory; The One who is satisfied receiving even small offerings like a leaf or a flower from his devotees; The One who is fierce; The One who is the measure of the year during which creatures exist and gather their experiences; The One who undertakes his task of creation, sustenance and destruction with ease; The abode of Seekers; The One who is most skilful.

vistāras sthāvara sthāṇuf
pramāṇam bīja-mavyayam |
arthoऽnartho mahākośo
mahābhogo mahādhanaha || 46 ||

The One who is so expansive as to include everyone and everything in the Universe; The One who is firm and motionless; The One who is the proof; The One who is the seed from which the whole Universe has arisen; The One who is worshipped by all; The One for whom nothing remains to be achieved or fulfilled; The One who is the sheath that covers everyone and everything; The giver of happiness and bliss to his devotees; The One who is of great wealth.

anirviṇṇas sthavishṭho sbhūr

dharmayūpo mahāmakhaha |

nakshatranemir-nakshatrī

kshamaha kshāmas samīhanaha || *47* ||

The One who has no desires to fulfil and therefore no occasion to feel or experience any disinterestedness; The One who is so large as to cover the whole Universe; The One without birth; The One who is the very essence of righteousness; The One for whom sacrifices are dedicated so that liberation from the cycle of births and deaths is achieved; The One around whom the sun, the moon and other planets move around; The One who is the Lord of the stars; The One who is ever patient; The One who remains unaffected by deluge; The One whose desires are auspicious.

yagña ijyo mahejyaścha
kratus satram satāngatihi |
sarvadarśī vimuktātmā
sarvagño gñānamuttamam || ***48*** ||

The One who is of the nature of *Yagna* (Rituals); The One who is invoked by *Yagnas*; The One who is most worshipped; The One who is the embodiment of ritualistic sacrifice; The One who protects the good; The One who is the refuge of all Seekers; The One who is the All-knower; The One who is the Ever-liberated Self; The One who is Omniscient; One who is the Supreme Knowledge in the form of Consciousness.

suvratas sumukhas sūkshmas
sughoshas sukhadas suhṛt |
manoharo jitakrodho
vīra bāhur-vidāraṇaha || 49 ||

The One who is steadfast in honouring his vow to protect and provide shelter to all his devotees; The One with a beautiful face; The One who is very subtle; The One who is of auspicious sound; The One who confers happiness; The One who is the friend of all living creatures; The One who is captivating; The One who has conquered anger; One with strong and mighty arms; The One who is a destroyer of those who live contrary to *Dharma* or Righteousness.

svāpanas svavaśo vyāpī
naikātmā naikakarmakṛt| |
vatsaro vatsalo vatsī
ratnagarbho dhaneśvaraha || 50 ||

The One who puts people to sleep; The One who has everything under his personal control; The One who is all-pervading; The One who is many-souled; The One who carries out many actions; The Abode of the Lord; The One who loves his devotees dearly; The One who is the father of all creatures in this Universe; The One who has wealth within himself; The Lord of wealth, including all objects of happiness.

dharmagub-dharmakṛd-dharmī
***sadasat-kshara-maksharam*||**
avigñātā sahasrāmśur
***vidhātā kṛtalakshaṇaha* || *51* ||**

One who protects *Dharma*; One who exemplifies *Dharma* by his own conduct; One who is the essence of *Dharma*; the all-pervading existence in all things and beings; The One who is an embodiment of all that exists and also that which is limited and temporary; The One who constantly undergoes change; The One who is immutable; The One who is not known to everyone; The One who is thousand rayed; The

One who supports the entire Universe; The One who is pure Consciousness which is the goal that is to be achieved for liberation (*Lakshana*).

gabhastinemis sattvasthas
simho bhūta maheśvaraha |
ādidevo mahādevo
deveśo devabhṛd-guruhu || 52 ||

The One who is the axis of all radiance; The One who is established in goodness, purity, virtuousness, etc. *or sattva*, which is the vehicle for the Supreme *Brahman* or Supreme Reality to express as God; The Lion, representing the form taken by Lord Vishnu to kill the demon Hiranyakashipu; The Lord of all beings; The First deity; The Great deity; The Lord of all *devas*; The One who is the protector and teacher (*guru*) of Indra, the king of the gods.

uttaro gopatir-goptā
gñānagamyaf purātanaha |
śarīra bhūtabhṛd bhoktā
kapīndro bhūridakshiṇaha || 53 ||

The One who is the foremost amongst all deities; The One who assumed the form of a cowherd (in his incarnation as Krishna); The protector of all living creatures; The One who is realized and attained only through pure knowledge or *jnana*; The One who pre-dates time; The One who nurses and nourishes the elements from which bodies are constituted; The One who is both the enjoyer and protector; The One who is the Lord of the monkeys (reference to Lord Rama), The One who gives away large gifts (*Dakshina*).

somapoऽmṛtapas somaf
purujit purusattamaha |
vinayo jayas satyasandho
dāśārhas sātvatām patihi || 54 ||

The One who consumes the soma juice (the receiver of all the offerings), The One who drinks the nectar; The One who is in the form of moonlight; The One who has won over many enemies; The one who is the greater among the greats; The One who shows supreme humility; The One who has conquered all matter; The embodiment of truth; The One who is born in Dasaarha race (*Yaadava-kula*) meaning Krishna; The Lord of the Satvat, referring to the devotees meditating with unwavering focus on the form of Lord Vishnu.

jīvo vinayitā sākshī

mukundoऽmita vikramaha |

ambhonidhi-ranantātmā

mahodadhi śayoऽntakaha || ***55*** ||

The One who remains as the limited ego (*Jeevah*); The One who is a witness to modesty and humility; The One who gives liberation; The One with immeasurable prowess; The One who is an ocean amongst lakes; The infinite Self beyond Time, Space and Matter; The One who reclines on the serpent *Adishesha* in the milky ocean of Vaikuntha; The One who is death and is the cause for ending.

ajo mahārhas svābhāvyo
jitāmitraf pramodanaha |
ānando nandano nandas
satyadharmā trivikramaha || 56 ||

The One who is Unborn- who is Eternal and has neither death nor decay; The One deserving of the highest worship; The One who is rooted in his true nature; The One who has conquered all his enemies, both within and without; The One who is ever blissful; The One who is pure bliss; The One who makes others blissful; The One who is freed from all worldly pleasures; The One who is embodiment of all *Dharmas*; The One who took the three steps (a reference to the *vamana* avatara of Lord Vishnu).

maharshih kapilāchāryah
kṛtagño medinīpatihi |
tripadas-tridaśādhyaksho
mahāśṛngah kṛtāntakṛt || 57 ||

The One who has manifested as Sage Kapila, the master of Vedic literature; The One who is both, the Universe that has been created and knower of all the objects in the Universe; The Lord of the Earth; The One who taken the three steps (a reference to the Lord's *vamana avatara*); The Lord of the three states of being... waking, dreaming and deep sleep; The One who is great horned (a reference to the *Matsya avatara* of Lord Vishnu), The God of destruction.

mahāvarāho govindas
susheṇah kanakāngadī |
guhyo gabhīro gahano
guptaś chakragadādharaha || 58 ||

The One who took the avatara of the great Boar (*Varaha*); The One who is to be known through the teachings and learnings of Vedanta; The One who has a charming army (*ganas*); The One with golden bright armlets; The One who is mysterious and whose realisation is a secret (*guhya*); The One who cannot be understood; The One who is impenetrable; The One who is concealed; The bearer of the discus (*chakra*) and mace (*gada*).

vedhās svāngoऽjitah kṛshṇo

dṛḍhas sankarshaṇoऽchyutaha |

varuṇo vāruṇo vṛkshaf

pushkarāksho mahāmanāha || 59 ||

The One who is the creator of the Universe; The One who is beautiful; The One who is vanquished by none; The One who was born to Vasudeva and Devaki as Krishna; The One who is firm; The One who absorbs the whole Universe into Himself; the One who knows no fall and always remains true to His essential nature; The One who like the sun at the end of the day disappears; The One who manifested Himself as Vasishta and Agastya; The One who is the Tree of Life; The One who has eyes as beautiful as the flowers of the Lotus; The One who has a great mind.

bhagavān bhagahāऽऽnandī

vanamālī halāyudhaha |

ādityo jyotirādityas

sahishṇur-gatisattamaha || 60 ||

The possessor of the six great glories (Wealth, Power, Dharma, Fame, Character, Knowledge and Dispassion, meaning *Bhagavān or the* Lord); The One who destroys during the deluge all the above six glories; The One who gives delight; The One who always wears the garland of leaves and flowers; The One who has the plough as a weapon (a reference to Balarama, the brother of Krishna); The One who was born as the son of Aditi and Kashyapa as *Vaamana*; The Supreme who is the essence of the brightness in the Sun;

The One who is calm; The Ultimate refuge for all devotees.

sudhanvā khaṇḍaparaśur

dāruṇo draviṇapradaha |

divas-spṛk - sarvadṛgvyāso

vāchaspatirayonijaha || 61 ||

The wielder of the bow '*Śārnga*'; the wielder of the axe–weapon, called '*Parasu*' (a reference to the '*Parasuram*' *avatara* of Lord Vishnu); The One who is merciless to the unrighteous; The One who gives wealth, including wealth of knowledge to his devotees; The One who reveals his True and Enormous Form (as He did to Arjuna in the Bhagavad Gita); The One who creates omniscient men; The One who is the master of all knowledge.

trisāmā sāmagas sāma

nirvāṇam bheshajam bhishak |

sanyāsakṛch chhamaś śānto

nishṭhā śāntif parāyaṇam ||62 ||

The One who has been glorified by the three *Saamas* (divine songs); The One who performs actions mentioned in the *Saama Veda*; The One who is *Saama Veda* himself; The One who is always liberated; The One who is the medicine for the disease of change; The One who is the physician or the cure for the disease; The One who helps and facilitates going through the fourth stage of renunciation, called the '*Samnyasa*'; The One who is ever calm; The One who is quiet within; The Abode of all beings both while living and during the deluge; One whose very nature is peace; The One who is the Supreme Goal for all seekers.

śubhāngaś śāntidas srashṭā
kumudah kuvaleśayaha |
gohito gopatir-goptā
vṛshabhāksho vṛshapriyaha || 63 ||

The One who has the most beautiful Form; The One who purifies the mind of his devotees and gives peace to all; the Creator of all beings; the reveller in the Earth; The One who reclines in the waters; The Protector of the cows; The One who is the husband of the Earth; The Protector of the Universe; The One who fulfils and grants the desires of his devotees; The One who delights in *Dharma*.

anivartī nivṛttātmā
samksheptā kshemakṛchchhivaha |
śrīvatsavakshāś śrīvāsaś
śrīpatiś śrīmatāmvaraha || ***64*** ||

One who never retreats; One who has conquered all the senses; One who absorbs unto Himself the entire Universe; The One who is a doer of good; The One who is auspicious; The One with the Sreevatsa mark on his chest; The One where *Sree* or Goddess Lakshmi resides; The One who is the husband of Goddess Lakshmi; The best amongst the ones who are prosperous.

śrīdaś śrīśaś śrīnivāsaś
śrīnidhiś śrīvibhāvanaha |
śrīdharaś śrīkaraś śreyaś
śrīmāl lokatrayāśrayaha || 65 ||

The One who grants wealth to all his sincere devotees; The Lord of the Goddess of wealth; The One who resides in purified hearts; The One who is the treasure-house of wealth; The One who is a distributor of wealth; The One who always carries Sree (Goddess of wealth) in His bosom; The One who bestows auspiciousness on those who meditate upon Him regularly; The One who is both the path and the goal to liberation; The One who possesses all glories, riches, and auspiciousness; The One who is the shelter of the three states of consciousness (wakefulness, sleep and deep sleep).

svakshas svangaś śatānando
nandir-jyotir-gaṇeśvaraha |
vijitātmā svidheyātmā
satkīrtiś chhinnasamśayaha || 66 ||

The One who is beautiful-eyed and beautiful-limbed; The One who manifests himself in different forms; The One who is always in a state of infinite bliss; The Lord of all the cosmos; The One who has conquered all sense organs; The One who is ever available to devotees; The One who is of pure fame; The One whose doubts are at rest or cleared.

udīrṇas sarvataśchakshu
***ranīśaś śāśvatasthiraha* |**
bhūśayo bhūshaṇo bhūtir
***viśokaś śokanāśanaha* || *67* ||**

The One who is infinite and superior to all beings; The One who has eyes everywhere; The One who has no Lord over Him; The One who is eternal and stable; The One who rests on the Earth (reference is to One who rested on the shores of the ocean, i.e. Lord Rama while going to Lanka); The One who adorns the world with his beautiful creations; The One who is the treasure house of all Glories; The One who is sorrow-less; The One who destroys all sorrows and grief of His devotees.

archishmā narchitah kumbho
viśuddhātmā viśodhanaha |
aniruddhospratirathaf
pradyumnosmitavikramaha || 68 ||

The One who is pure Consciousness and the source of all Light; The One who is constantly the object of worship; The One in whom the whole Universe is contained like in a pot; The One having the purest Soul; The One who is the great purifier; The One who cannot be ever defeated; The One who is never challenged by any enemies; The One who is very rich; The One who is of immeasurable prowess.

kālaneminihā vīraś
śauriś śūrajaneśvaraha |
trilokātmā trilokeśah
keśavah keśihā harihi || 69 ||

The One who slew the Asura, Kalanemi; '*Kala*' also means Time, and therefore it could also mean 'The One who destroys Time' by transcending it as the Self; The One who is a heroic victor; The One born in the Shurasena clan; The One who is Lord of the courageous; The Lord of the three states of Consciousness namely, Wakefulness, Sleep and Deep Sleep; The One who is the essence of existence; The One who has long hair, namely, Krishna; The destroyer of the Asura, *Kesi*; The One who destroys all doubts, confusion and inner conflicts.

kāmadevah kāmapālah
kāmī kāntah kṛtāgamaha |
anirdeśyavapur-vishṇur
vīroऽnanto dhanañjayaha || 70 ||

The One who is the Beloved Lord; The One who fulfils desires of His true devotees; The One who has fulfilled all His desires; The One who is of Enchanting Form; The One who is the author of the scriptures; The One who cannot be described;

The One who is all-pervading; The One who is valiant; The One who is Infinite; The One who has gained lot of wealth and prowess through his conquests, like Dhananjaya (Arjuna), (In Gita, Krishna says, 'I am Dhananjaya, among the sons of Pandu').

bramhaṇyo bramhakṛd bramhā
bramha bramhavivardhanaha |
bramhavid brāmhaṇo bramhī
bramhagño brāmhaṇapriyaha || 71 ||

The One who is a great friend of the learned; The One who lives in Truth; The One who is a Creator; The One who is all-pervading; The One who increases knowledge of all Vedas and Truth; The One who knows the Brahman or Supreme Reality; The One who has self-realised through austerities and learning; The One who is with Truth and Knowledge; The One who lives in a state of Supreme Consciousness; The One who loves people who have self-realised.

mahākramo mahākarmā
mahātejā mahoragaha |
mahākratur-mahāyajvā
mahāyagño mahāhavihi || 72 ||

The One with great steps (a reference to the *Vamana avatara* of Lord Vishnu); The One who performs great deeds; The One who is very bright; The One who is the "Great Serpent" (In the Bhagavad Gita Krishna says, 'Among the serpents, I am Vasuki'); The realisation of the Supreme, through the "Great Sacrifice" (the reference here is to the complete sacrifice or shedding of one's ego); The One who performs great *yagnas* (sacrifices): (In the Bhagavad Gita, Krishna tells Arjuna, 'I am among the *Yajnas*, the *Japa Yajna*', which is basically an exhortation to win the divine Grace of the Lord with unwavering devotion or *Bhakti*), 'The Great offering' means all the things offered to the sacred fire.

stavyas stavapriyas stotram
stutis stotā raṇapriyaha |
pūrṇaf pūrayitā puṇyaf
puṇyakīrti-ranāmayaha || *73* ||

The One who is the object of all praise; The One who is invoked by loving chants of devotees; The One who is also the process of chanting hymns; The act of praise; The One who chants praises of the Lord; The One who is a lover of battles; The One who is complete in all respects; The One who is a fulfiller; The One who is most auspicious and Holy; The One who attains fame by glorifying Lord Vishnu; The One who has neither mental nor physical diseases.

Manojavas tīrthakaro
vasuretā vasupradaha |
vasuprado vāsudevo
vasurvasumanā havihi || *74* ||

The One who is very ready to reach his devotees quickly; The One who is the ancient teacher of all forms of knowledge; The One whose essence is golden and from whom the entire Universe emerged; The One who gives wealth freely; The One who gives salvation; The One who is the son of Vasudeva, namely Krishna; The One who is the refuge for everyone; The One who is omnipresent; The One who is the oblation Himself.

sadgatis satkṛtis sattā
sadbhūtis satparāyaṇaha |
śūraseno yaduśreshṭhas
sannivāsas suyāmunaha || 75 ||

The Goal of all-pious devotees; The One who is full of good actions; The One who is pure experience; The One who has rich glories and manifested himself in various incarnations; The highest state attainable by holy persons who always pursue the path of Truth; The One who has heroic and valiant armies; The best among the Yadava clan; The One who is an abode of those who have self-realised; The One surrounded by the residents who live on the banks of the Yamuna (reference to Krishna).

bhūtāvāso vāsudevas

sarvāsunilayoऽnalaha |

darpahā darpadoऽdṛpto

durdharoऽthāऽparājitaha || *76* ||

The abode of all creatures; The all-pervading One; The One who resides in everything; The One who is full of unlimited Glories; The destroyer of pride in evil minded people; The granter of pride to the righteous or with *sattva guna*; The One who is ever blissful; The One who is hard to perceive; The One who can never be vanquished.

viśvamūrtir-mahāmūrtir

dīptamūrti-ramūrtimān |

anekamūrti-ravyaktaś

śatamūrtiś śatānanaha || *77* ||

The One who is in the gross Universe; The One who is both, the Universe as well as its Creator; The One who is luminous; The One without a form; The One with many manifestations (*Avataras*); The One who is indescribable; The One with hundreds of manifestations; The One with hundreds of faces.

eko naikas savah kah kim
yattat padamanuttamam |
lokabandhur-lokanātho
mādhavo bhaktavatsalaha || ***78*** ||

The One without a second; The One who while being present in all living creatures, also represents plurality and is therefore also expressed as "the many"; The One who is in the nature of sacrifice; The One who is blissful; The One who is the object of enquiry and is phrased as the question 'What'; The One who is self-existent; That which encompasses the world of plurality; The One who is an unequalled state of perfection; The One who is a friend of the whole world; The One who is a Lord of the world; The

One who was born in the family of Madhu; The One with unbounded love for his devotees.

suvarṇavarṇo hemāngo
varāngaśchandanāngadī |
vīrahā vishamaś śūnyo
ghṛtāśī-rachala-śchalaha || 79 ||

The One who is golden coloured; The One who has limbs of gold; The One with beautiful limbs; The One who has attractive armlets; The destroyer of valiant heroes; The One who has no equal; The state of void where Pure Consciousness exists above and beyond all other states of Consciousness; The One who does not require good wishes from anyone; The One who is all-pervading and omnipresent; The One who is always moving.

amānī mānado mānyo
lokasvāmī trilokadhṛk |
sumedhā medhajo dhanyas
satyamedhā dharādharaha || 80 ||

The One who knows his own divine nature; The One who honours all his true devotees; The One who is most respected and honoured; The One who is Lord of the Universe; The One who supports the three worlds; The One who has pure Intelligence; The One who is born out of sacrifices (*Yagna*); The One endowed with the future; The One whose intelligence never fails; The One who is the sole support of the Earth.

tejovṛsho dyutidharas
sarvaśastrabhṛtām varaha |
pragraho nigraho vyagro
naikaśṛngo gadāgrajaha || 81 ||

The One who showers radiance; The One who bears effulgence; The One who is best among those who wield weapons; The One who receives all offerings; The One who is a destroyer of ego; The One who is always engaged in fulfilling the devotees' desires; The One who has many horns (reference is to the four states of Consciousness, namely, Wake, Dream, Deep Sleep and Pure

Consciousness); The One who was the elder brother of Gada, viz, Krishna.

chaturmūrtiś śchaturbāhuś
śchaturvyūhaś śchaturgatihi |
chaturātmā chaturbhāvaś
chaturvedavidekapāt || 82 ||

The One who is four-formed (According to the Puranas, Lord assumed different colours during his manifestations in different *Yugas* – white in *Satya yuga*, red in *Treta yuga*, yellow in *Dvaapara yuga* and black in *Kali yuga*); The One having four hands; The One who expresses himself in four kinds of formations with Himself in the centre as a Controller; the ultimate goal of people of all four *varnas*; The One who is free from all aspects of Ego; The One who is the source of the four *varnas (Brahmana, Kshatriya, Vaishya and Shudra)*, of the four stages of life (*Brahmacharya, Grihastha, Vanaprastha and Sanyasa*), and the four human aspirations, namely, *Dharma* (Righteousness), *Artha* (Wealth), *Kaama* (Pleasure) and *Moksha*

(Spiritual Liberation); The One who is the knower of all four Vedas; The One who supports the entire Universe by only a fraction of His part.

samāvartoऽnivṛttātmā

durjayo duratikramaha |

durlabho durgamo durgo

durāvāso durārihā || 83 ||

The turner of the wheel of life; The One whose mind is above all sense indulgences; The One who is invincible; The One who cannot be disobeyed; The One who is attained with a lot of effort; The One who is hard to reach; The One who can be reached only after crossing many hurdles; The One who resides in the mind after much struggle; The One who detects and destroys the devil inside us.

śubhāngo lokasārangas.

sutantus tantuvardhanaha |

indrakarmā mahākarmā

kṛtakarmā kṛtāgamaha || 84 ||

The One with enchanting limbs; The One who is realised with the cosmic syllable Om; The One who is beautifully expanded; The One who fosters creation; The One who performs glorious and auspicious actions; The One who accomplishes great activities like creating and sustaining an entire Universe; The One who has fulfilled all His activities; The One who is the author of Vedas.

udbhavas sundaras sundo
ratnanābhas sulochanaha |
arko vājasanaś śṛngī
jayantas sarvavijjayī || 85 ||

The One who is the springboard of creation; The One with unparalleled beauty; The One with great compassion; The One with the beautiful jewel-like Navel; The One with enchanting eyes; The One who is in the form of the Sun; The One who is the giver of food; The One with a horn (a reference to the *Matsya avatara* of Lord Vishnu), the conqueror of all enemies; The One who is omniscient and ever victorious.

suvarṇabindu rakshobhyas

sarvavāgīśvareśvaraha |

mahāhrado mahāgarto

mahābhūto mahānidhihi || 86 ||

The One with limbs radiant like gold; The One who never gets rattled or flustered; The Lord of speech; The One who is like a great body of water; The One like a great chasm (a reference to the *Maya* or illusions of the Lord); The source from which *Panch Bhootas* or five elements arose; The One who is Himself the Great Treasure.

kumudah kundarah kundaf

parjanyaf pāvanoऽnilaha|

amṛtāśo ऽmṛtavapus

sarvagñas sarvatomukhaha || 87 ||

The One who gladdens the Earth; The One who tore the Earth in his *avatara* as the *Varaha* or

Boar; The One who as *Parashurama* gave away the Earth to Sage Kashyapa; The One who causes rain; The One who is the Supreme Purifier; The One who flows like the breeze; The One who consumes *Amrit* (Nectar); The One whose form is immortal; The One who is omniscient; The One who has his face turned in all directions.

sulabhas suvratas siddhaś
śatrujich-chhatrutāpanaha|
nyagrodhoऽdumbaroऽśvatthaś
chāṇūrāndhra nishūdanaha || 88 ||

The One who is readily available; The One who has taken the most auspicious forms; The One who is perfection itself; The One who is ever victorious; The One who scorches his enemies; The One who is there within each one of us but remains veiled; The One who is the nourisher of all creatures; The One who is the immortal Tree of Life; The slayer of Chaanoora, the fierce and mighty wrestler (a reference is to Lord Vishnu's *avatara* as Krishna).

sahasrārchis saptajihvas
saptaidhās saptavāhanaha |
amūrti ranaghoxchintyo
bhayakṛd-bhayanāśanaha || 89 ||

The One who has thousands of rays; The One with seven kinds of tongues ('tongues of flames'), which illumine the world of perception in us, namely, two eyes, two ears, two nostrils and the mouth; The One who is the brightness in the 'seven tongues of flames'; The One with a vehicle of seven horses; The One who is formless; The One who is sinless; The One who cannot be comprehended by man's mind and intellect; The One who is a terror to the evil-minded; The One who is a destroyer of all fear.

aṇur-bṛhat-kṛśas sthūlo
guṇabhṛn nirguṇo mahān |
adhṛtas svadhṛtas svāsyaf
prāgvamśo vamśavardhanaha || 90 ||

The One who is the subtlest; The One who is Greater than the greatest; The One who is lean; The One who is the fattest; The One who supports and expresses through the three *gunas* (*Rajas*: to create; *Sattva*: to preserve; *Tamas*: to destroy); The One without any properties; The One who is Supreme; The One who supports all but not requiring support from anyone; The One who is self-supported; The One who has a bright face; The One who has an ancient ancestry; The One who multiplies his family of descendants.

bhārabhṛt-kathito yogī
yogīśas sarvakāmadaha |
āśramaś śramaṇaha kshāmas
suparṇo vāyuvāhanaha || ***91*** ||

The One who carries the entire load of the Universe; The One who is glorified and extolled in the Vedas; The One who can be realised through *yoga*; The One who is the king of all those who have self-realised; The One who fulfils the desires of his devotees; The One who is Himself a state of peace, joy, quietness and bliss; The One who persecutes worldly people driven by senses; The One who destroys everything during the final deluge; The 'Golden Leaf' (In the Bhagavad Gita, the world is denoted by the Asvattha tree while its beautiful leaves are the Vedas signifying knowledge); The One who is responsible for the movement of the wind.

dhanurdharo dhanurvedo
daṇḍo damayitā damaha |
aparājitas sarvasaho
niyantāsniyamosyamaha || 92 ||

The One who is the wielder of the great bow; The One who is the master of archery; The One who punishes the wicked; The One who is the regulator of this Universe; The One who is the embodiment of control and discipline; The One who is invincible; The One who carries the entire Universe; The One who has none above him to control Him; The One who is not subject to the laws of anyone else; The One who has no death.

sattvavān sāttvikas
satyas satyadharmaparāyaṇaha |
abhiprāyaf priyārhosrhaf
priyakṛt prītivardhanaha || 93 ||

The One who is full of heroism and powers; The One who is full of *sattvic* qualities, viz., peace, calmness, tranquility, etc.; The One who is the embodiment of Truth; The abode of Truth and Righteousness; The One who is sought by all; The One deserving of love from everyone, The One deserving of worship by everyone; The One who is ever happy to fulfil the wishes of his devotees; The One who enhances the joy of his devotees.

vihāyasagatir-jyotis
suruchir-hutabhugvibhuhu |
ravir-virochanas sūryas
savitā ravilochanaha || 94 ||

The One who moves through space; The One who is effulgent with His own light; The One of great glory; The One who receives all offerings of the Vedic rituals; The One who is all-pervading; The One who absorbs everything like the Sun; The One who shines in different forms; The One of great energy; The One who brings forth from Himself the entire Universe; The One whose eyes are the Sun.

Ananto hutabhug bhoktā

sukhado naikajo'grajaha ।

anirviṇṇas sadāmarshī

***lokādhishṭhāna madbhutaha* || *95* ||**

The One who is endless; The One who accepts the things poured into the sacred fire during the rituals; The One who protects; The One who gives the experience of bliss or *moksha* (liberation from the cycle of birth, death and rebirth) to his devotees; The One who manifests Himself repeatedly in different forms to serve his devotees; The One who was first-born; The One who feels no disappointments; The One who is ever forgiving to the faults of his devotees; The One who is a substratum or foundation for the Universe made up of things and beings; The One who is wondrous.

sanāt sanātanatamah

kapilah kapi-ravyayaha |

svastidas svastikṛt-svasti

svastibhuk svasti dakshiṇaha || 96 ||

The One who is not conditioned by Time and Space; The One who is most ancient; The One who shines like a coppery-red flame; The One who drinks water by one's rays; The One in whom the entire Universe merges during the deluge; The One who grants well-being; The One who grants auspiciousness; The One who is the source of all auspiciousness; The One who relishes well-being; The One who is very efficient in distributing auspiciousness.

araudrah kuṇḍalī chakrī
vikramyūrjitaśāsanaha |
śabdātigaś śabdasahaś
śiśiraś śarvarīkaraha || 97 ||

The One without any negative traits; The One who wears the earring, called *Makara-Kundala*; The wielder of the discus called *Sudarshana* (auspicious vision); The One who is more daring than anyone; The One who commands and administers with His hand; The One who is indescribable; The One invoked by Vedic incantations; The One who is an embodiment of coolness and shelter for all those suffering from the rigours of *samsara* (cycle of birth, death and rebirth); The One who creates darkness.

akrūraf peśalo daksho
dakshiṇaha kshamiṇām varaha |
vidvattamo vītabhayaf
puṇyaśravaṇakīrtanaha || 98 ||

The One who is never cruel; The One who is Supremely soft; The One who is very competent; The One who is very benevolent; The One with a great sense of forgiveness; The One endowed with great wisdom; The One who is fearless; The One whose glory when heard or chanted bestows virtue.

uttāraṇo dushkṛtihā
puṇyo dus-svapnanāśanaha |
vīrahā rakshaṇas santo
jīvanaf paryavasthitaha || ***99*** ||

The One who uplifts; The One who destroys bad actions; The One who purifies the heart of his devotees; The One who destroys all bad dreams; The One who liberates; The One who is the protector of the Universe; The One who is pious; The One who is the life-giving energy of all creatures; The One who is situated everywhere.

anantarūpoऽ***nantaśrīr***

jitamanyur-bhayāpahaha |

chaturaśro gabhīrātmā

vidiśo vyādiśo diśaha || 100 ||

The One with infinite forms; The One full of infinite glories; The One who has conquered anger; The One who drives away fear; The One who deals justly with all; The One who is very profound; The One who bestows appropriate rewards; The One who issues appropriate commands; The One who advises and gives knowledge.

anādir-bhūrbhuvo lakshmīs

suvīro ruchirāngadaha |

janano janajanmādir

bhīmo bhīmaparākramaha || 101 ||

The One without a beginning; The One who is the very substratum of Earth; The One who is the bestower of all that is auspicious; The One who manifests himself in glorious ways; The One who wears shining shoulder caps; The One who delivers all living creatures; The One who is the sole cause of the birth of all living creatures; The One whose form is fearsome and frightening to the sinners; The One whose power and courage is frightening to his enemies.

ādhāranilayo dhātā
pushpahāsaf prajāgaraha |
ūrdhvagas satpathāchāraf
prāṇadaf praṇavaf paṇaha || 102 ||

The One who is the fundamental sustainer; The One who is the Supreme Controller; The One who shines like an opening flower; The One who is ever-awake; The One who is on the top of everything; The One who walks the path of Truth; The One who bestows life; The One who is the cosmic sound of "OM"; The One who is the Supreme Manager of the Universe.

pramāṇam prāṇanilayaf
prāṇabhṛt prāṇajīvanaha |
tattvam tattvavidekātmā
janmamṛtyujarātigaha || 103 ||

The One whose very form is the Vedas; The One who is the substratum for all activities in all living creatures; The One who sustains life amongst all organisms; The One who keeps all living beings alive with the divine touch of breath; The One which is the essence; The One who has realised the Self; The One who is the One Self; The One who knows no change in Himself and is subject to neither birth nor death.

bhūrbhuvas svastarustāras
savitā prapitāmahaha |
yagño yagñapatir-yajvā
yagñāngo yagñavāhanaha || 104 ||

The One who is the sap in the Tree-of-life; The One who is the boatman who can row his devotees across the cycle of birth and rebirth; The One who is the father of all; The One who is the father of even the creator, Brahma; The One whose very nature is *Yagna (vedic rituals)*; The One who is the Lord of all *yagnas*; The One who performs *yagna*; The One whose parts are employed in *yagnas*; The One who fulfils *yajnas* precisely, the way the Vedic instructions want them to be done.

yagñabhṛd yagñakṛd yagñī
yagñabhug yagñasādhanaha |
yagñāntakṛd yagñaguhya
manna-mannāda eva cha || ***105*** ||

The One who is a protector and supporter of *yagnas*; The One who creates and facilitates the process of *yagna*; The One who is the constant enjoyer of *yagnas*; The One who is the recipient of all offerings in a *yagna*; The One who ensures the success of a *yagna*; The One who performs the concluding act in all *yagnas*; The One who is the profound truth in a *yagna*; The One who is the embodiment of nourishment; The One who bestows nourishment.

ātmayonis svayamjāto

vaikhānas sāmagāyanaha |

devakīnandanas srashṭā

kshitīśaf pāpanāśanaha || 106 ||

The One who is the cause for Himself; The One who is self-created; The One who dug through the Earth (a reference to 'Varaha' *avatara* of Lord Vishnu); The One who sings the *Sama* songs; The One who was born to Devaki as Krishna; The Creator of all the worlds; The One who is the Lord of the Earth; The One who is the destroyer of evil thoughts and sins.

śankhabhṛn nandakī chakrī

śārngadhanvā gadādharaha |

rathāngapāṇi rakshobhyas

sarvapraharaṇāyudhaha || 107 ||

śrī sarvapraharaṇāyudha om nama iti |

The One who bears the divine conch, "*Panchajanya*"; The One who wields the sword, "*Nandaka*"; The One who wields the discus, "*Sudharshana*" ('Auspicious Vision'); The One who wields the divine bow, "*Śārnga*"; The One who wields the divine mace, "*Kaumodakee*"; The One who wields the chariot wheel in His hand; The One whose calm and peace cannot be disturbed; The One who has all the implements for all kinds of warfare apart from what is mentioned here.

[2]vanamālī gadī śārngī
śankhī chakrī cha nandakī |
śrīmān nārāyaṇo vishṇur
vāsudevoऽbhirakshatu || 108 ||

---

[2] In several commentaries of the Vishnu Sahasranama, the shlokas end with shloka 107 or the 1000th nāma, namely 'sarV()prahar()ṇāyudh()ha'. However, since some other commentaries go beyond to shloka 108, the same has been reproduced and addressed here.

śrī vāsudevoऽbhirakshatu om nama iti

The One garlanded in forest flowers, who wields a mace, a bow, a conch, a wheel, and a sword. That Lord, accompanied by the Goddess of wealth, known as Narayana, Vishnu and Vasudeva, May He bestow protection!

Chapter - 4

Phalashruti

(Fruits of Listening)

Phalashruti in Sanskrit is made up of two words '*Phala*', meaning fruit, and '*shruti*', meaning listening, which translates thereby to 'fruits of listening'. In the case of Vishnu Sahasranama, Phalashruti appears as a few shlokas at the very end ('*uttara bhāgam*') of the main Vishnu Sahasranama, which spells out the benefits of chanting or listening (here, it may be noted that even **listening** to the chanting of Sahasranama is considered good enough for a devotee) to the thousand names of Lord Vishnu on a daily basis. There are shlokas in the Phalashruti where Bhishma, Veda Vyasa, Arjuna, Krishna, Parvati (wife of Shiva and an embodiment of Shakti), Shiva, Brahma and Sanjaya (the Advisor of

Dhritarashtra blessed with a telescopic vision and extraordinary powers of hearing) have given their views or narratives on the Lord.

itīdam kīrtanīyasya
keśavasya mahātmanaha |
nāmnām sahasram divyānā
maśesheṇa prakīrtitam| || (1) ||

(These are Shri Bhishma's words):

Thus, the thousand divine names of Bhagavan Keshava, the Supreme who is pre-eminently worthy of being praised, have been sung in their entirety.

ya idam śṛṇuyānnityam
yaśchāpi parikīrtayet||
nāśubham prāpnuyāt kiñchit
soऽmutreha cha mānavaha || (2) ||

Nothing inauspicious shall ever befall the one who devoutly listens to the recital of this Sahasranama Stotra daily and the one who recites it, wherever it may be, whether in this world or in the worlds beyond.

vedāntago brāmhaṇas syāt
kshatriyo vijayī bhavet |
vaiśyo dhanasamṛddhas syāch
chhūdras sukhamavāpnuyāt || (3) ||

If a person who chants these names is a Brahmin, he will attain the knowledge of the Vedanta; if a Kshatriya, he will become a victorious warrior; if a Vaishya, he will acquire immense wealth, and if a shudra, he will remain happy.

dharmārthī prāpnuyād dharma
marthārthī chārthamāpnuyāt |
kāmāna vāpnuyāt kāmī
prajārthī chāpnuyāt prajām || (4) ||

If a person recites the holy names while wanting to follow Dharma, he will achieve it; if he is desirous of wealth, he will get it; if he is after the pleasures of life, he will get them; if he wants progeny, he will get it. Those who recite the thousand names of the Lord shall reap the desired fruits without fail.

bhaktimān yas sadotthāya
śuchis tadgatamānasaha |
sahasram vāsudevasya
nāmnāmetat prakīrtayet || ***(5)*** ||

The devotee who gets up early in the morning and recites the thousand names of the Lord will be rid of any disease he is suffering from. He who is in bondage shall be liberated. He who is affected by fear will overcome it, and he who is in difficulties will be free of them.

yaśaf prāpnoti vipulam
gñātiprādhānyameva cha |
achalām śriyamāpnoti
śreyaf prāpnotyanuttamam| || ***(6)*** ||

He gains a great reputation and is reckoned as the foremost amongst his kith and kin. He acquires abundant wealth and keeps it intact while he enjoys everlasting bliss and salvation in the other world.

na bhayam kvachidāpnoti
vīryam tejaścha vindati |
bhavatyarogo dyutimān
balarūpa guṇānvitaha || (7) ||

Free from fear and sickness, the chanter acquires valour, power and strength and is endowed with a healthy body, noble traits and dazzling brilliance.

rogārto muchyate rogād
baddho muchyeta bandhanāt |
bhayān-muchyeta bhītastu
muchyetāpanna āpadaha || (8) ||

The one afflicted by sickness will get rid of it; the one in shackles of sorts will get disentangled, while the one stricken by fear will become free from it, and the one beset with difficulties will get absolved of them.

durgāṇyatitaratyāśu
purushaf purushottamam |
stuvannāma sahasreṇa
nityam bhakti samanvitaha || (9) ||

That person who praises the Supreme Being Purushottama with devotion by reciting His Thousand names daily, will overcome all difficulties.

vāsudevāśrayo martyo
vāsudeva parāyaṇaha |
sarvapāpa viśuddhātmā
yāti bramha sanātanam| || (10) ||

The one, who seeks out Lord Vasudeva, looking upon Him as the highest goal to be attained, gets cleansed of all sins. With such a purified mind, the chanter attains the eternal Brahman.

na vāsudeva bhaktānā
maśubham vidyate kvachit |
janma mṛtyu jarā vyādhi
bhayam naivopajāyate || (11) ||

Nothing ever befalls the devotees of Vasudeva, nor do they have any fear of the cycle of birth, death, disease and old age.

imam stavamadhīyānaś
śraddhā bhakti samanvitaha |
yujyetātma sukhakshānti
śrīdhṛti smṛti kīrtibhihi || (12) ||

The one who chants this hymn with zeal and devotion is blessed with the happy realisation of the essential nature of the Self, besides the qualities of serenity, mental stability, unfailing memory, great fame and wealth.

na krodho na cha mātsaryam
na lobho nāśubhāmatihi |
bhavanti kṛta puṇyānām
bhaktānām purushottame || (13) ||

Neither anger nor jealousy, neither avarice nor unholy thoughts taint the minds of true devotees of Purushottama, who have to their credit, many a virtuous deed.

dyaus sa chandrārka nakshatra
kham diśo bhūrmahodadhihi |
vāsudevasya vīryeṇa
vidhṛtāni mahātmanaha || (14) ||

The firmament, the Moon, the Sun and Stars, the Sky, the directions, the Earth and the vast Ocean are but borne by the valour of the great Lord Vasudeva.

sasurāsura gandharvam
sayakshoraga rākshasam |
jagadvaśe vartatedam
kṛshṇasya sa charācharam| || (15) ||

This world, with all its contents, the sentient beings and non-sentient things, the gods, the asuras and gandharvas, the yakshas, nagas and rakshasas, is under the supreme control of Sri Krishna.

indriyāṇi manobuddhis
sattvam tejo balam dhṛtihi |
vāsudevātma kānyāhuhu
kshetram kshetragña eva cha || (16) ||

The several sense organs, the mind, the intellect, the power, the strength, the firmness, as well as the body as a whole, and the individual souls - all of them have Vasudeva as their *Atma* or Inner Soul.

sarvāgamānā māchāraf
prathamam parikalpate |
āchāra prabhavo dharmo
dharmasya prabhurachyutaha || (17) ||

Right conduct has been laid down as the most important, the foremost amongst all the *Dharmas* revealed by the *Shastras*. Right conduct is the one that gives rise to *Dharmas*. Bhagavan Achyuta is the deity propitiated by *Dharma*, who not only helps in one's adherence to *Dharma* but also awards the fruits thereof.

ṛshayaf pitaro devā
mahābhūtāni dhātavaha |
jangamā jangamam chedam
jagannārāyaṇodbhavam || (18) ||

All the sages, the ancestors, all the *devas*, all the five *mahabhutas* or elements, all the pleasures, all the mobile beings, and all immobile things, comprising the entire Universe, have all emanated from the Great Narayana.

yogogñānam tathā sānkhyam
vidyāś śilpādikarma cha |
vedāś śāstrāṇi vigñānam
etat sarvam janārdanāt || (19) ||

The knowledge of yoga, the Science of Sankhya (the philosophical basis of realising self or self-knowledge), the treasure of knowledge, the divine art of sculpture, and all the Vedas and science came from Janardhana.

eko vishṇur-mahad-bhūtam
pṛthagbhūtā nyanekaśaha |
trīllokān vyāpya bhūtātmā
bhunkte viśvabhugavyayaha || (20) ||

Shri Maha Vishnu is ONE and has an immense form, yet he divides Himself and exists in all beings in many different ways. He pervades the three worlds and rules over all of them. He enjoys them and consumes them. He has no death or decay.

Lord Vishnu displaying His Vishvarupa (huge) form to Arjuna on the battlefield of Kurukshetra

imam stavam bhagavato
vishṇor-vyāsena kīrtitam |
paṭhedya ichchhet-purushaś
śreyaf prāptum sukhāni cha || (21) ||

He who desires fame and pleasure should chant these verses of Bhagavan Vishnu, composed by the great sage Vyasa.

viśveśvara majam devam
jagataf prabhumavyayam|
bhajanti ye pushkarāksham
na te yānti parābhavam || (22) ||

The one with Lotus eyes who is unborn is the Supreme Deity, the sovereign Lord of the Universe and the cause and dissolution of the Universe. Those who sing his praise will never meet with any setback, discomfiture or disrespect.

(There is a reiteration and repeat of the above for Sage Vyasa adds at the end - perhaps for emphasis):

"Never do they meet with any disrespect. Never do they meet with any disrespect".

Arjuna uvācha

padmapatra viśālāksha

padmanābha surottama |

bhaktānā manuraktānām

trātā bhava janārdana || (23) ||

Oh, Lord Vishnu, your eyes are large like that of the Lotus leaf; You have a Lotus coming out of your Navel; You are the greatest amongst the *Devas*; Please protect your ardent devotees who are engaged in their devotion for you (It may be noted here that Arjuna has pleaded for protection from the Lord for ALL his devotees).

śrībhagavān uvācha

yo mām nāma sahasreṇa

stotumichchati pāṇḍava |

soऽhamekena ślokena

stuta eva na samśayaha || (24) ||

stuta eva na samśaya om nama iti |

The Lord says:

He who likes to sing my praise, Oh Arjuna, using these thousand names, should know that I would be satisfied by his chanting of even one shloka. Of that, let there be no doubt! Of that, let there be no doubt! (This is a repeat for the sake of emphasis by the Lord). Salutations to the Lord!

vyāsa uvācha

vāsanād vāsudevasya

vāsitam bhuvanatrayam |

sarvabhūta nivāsoऽsi

vāsudeva namoऽstu te ||

śrīvāsudeva namostuta om nama iti || (25) ||

Sage Vyasa says:

The three worlds have become habitable only because Bhagavan Vasudeva is present in all three.

Salutations to Vasudeva, who is the abode for all beings! (This is repeated again for greater emphasis).

pārvatyuvācha

kenopāyena laghunā

vishṇor-nāma sahasrakam |

paṭhyate paṇḍitair-nityam

śrotumichchhāmyaham prabho || (26) ||

Goddess Parvati asks Lord Shiva:

Oh Lord, is there any simple and quick method by which learned people are able to recite these thousand names of Lord Vishnu every day? If so, I would like to hear about it!

īśvara uvācha

śrīrāma rāma rāmeti

rame rāme manorame |

sahasranāma tattulyam

rāmanāma varānane ||

***śrīrāma nāma varānana om nama iti** || (27) ||*

Lord Shiva says (in response):

Oh, beautiful lady, I derive pleasure by always chanting the Rama Nama repeatedly, and uttering the Rama Nama even once is equivalent to reciting all the thousand *nāmas*. (The salutation part at the end, viz. '*Sri Rama nama varanana om nama iti*' is for further emphasis. It was a customary mode of using such a phrase to reiterate a point or even a salutation).

Bramhovācha

namoऽstvanantāya sahasramūrtaye

sahasrapādākshi śirorubāhave |

sahasranāmne purushāya śāśvate

sahasrakoṭi yugadhāriṇe namaha ||

śrī sahasrakoṭi yugadhāriṇe nama om nama iti || (28) ||

(This is a prayer from Lord Brahma to Lord Vishnu):

Brahma says:

Salutations to the endless and Immortal One who has thousands of Forms, thousands of feet, thousands of eyes and thousands of arms. Salutations to Him who has thousands of Names, who is the soul in all beings and who is permanent. Salutations to Him who keeps creating billions of *yugas* or Time Cycles.

sañjaya uvācha

yatra yogeśvarah kṛshṇo
yatra pārtho dhanurdharaha |
tatra śrīr-vijayo bhūtir
dhruvā nītir-matir-mama || (29) ||

(The above is a Shloka from Chapter 18 of the Bhagavad Gita. Sanjaya says this to Dhritarashtra at the conclusion of the dialogue between Arjuna and Krishna)

Sanjaya says:

Where Krishna, the King of Yogas, and where the wielder of bow Arjuna are there, it is there that will exist all the good, all the victory, all the fame and all the justice in this world.

śrī bhagavān uvācha

ananyāś chintayanto mām

ye janāf paryupāsate |

teshām nityābhiyuktānām

yogakshemam vahāmyaham || (30) ||

(The above Shloka is from Chapter 9 of the Bhagavad Gita): Shri Bhagavan says:

For those who are constantly engaged in my worship with single-minded focus, I carry with me what they lack and preserve what they have.

paritrāṇāya sādhūnām
vināśāya cha dushkṛtām| |
dharma samsthāpanārthāya
sambhavāmi yuge yuge || (31) ||

(The above shloka is from Chapter 4 of the Bhagavad Gita):

To take care of *Dharma*, to protect those who are good, and to destroy all who are bad, I will take birth in every age.

ārtā vishaṇṇāś śithilāścha bhītāh
ghoreshu cha vyādhishu vartamānāha |
sankīrtya nārāyaṇa śabdamātram
vimukta duhkhās sukhino bhavantu || (32) ||

Those afflicted by distress or grief or shattered by confusion due to fear or tormented by diseases - in each of these cases, if they just call out the name of 'Narayana', they will not only get rid of all their troubles but also attain everlasting happiness.

kāyena vāchā manasendri yairvā

buddhyātmanā vā prakṛtes svabhāvāt |

karomi yadyat-sakalam parasmai

nārāyaṇāyeti samarpayāmi || (33) ||

Whatever I do with my body, speech, mind, with other senses of my body, with my intellect and soul or with my innate natural tendencies, I dedicate everything to Lord Narayana.

Conclusion

There are several Sahasranamas dedicated to different deities. The Lalitha Sahasranama is dedicated to Mother Lalitha Devi, one of the forms of Goddess Durga. This Sahasranama is more commonly chanted and listened to in South India. There is the Kali Sahasranama, which is, as suggested by the name, dedicated to Goddess Kali and is invoked most commonly in Bengal. Then there is the Ganesha Sahasranama, which is invoked across several temples and especially by those who follow the Ganapatya tradition of Hinduism, which believe Lord Ganesha to be the Supreme deity. The Bhavani Nāma Sahasra Stuti is commonly chanted by the Pandits of Kashmir. However, the Vishnu Sahasranama, alongside the Shiva Sahasranama, remains by far the most popular of the Sahasranamas in the entire Hindu pantheon.

What is it, one might ask, that makes the Vishnu Sahasranama so very unique? The status of Lord Vishnu as the Supreme Being who is the Controller, Regulator, Creator, Nourisher, Sustainer and Destroyer of this Universe and its creations is in itself a compelling reason for the Vishnu Sahasranama to remain an extremely popular chant amongst the followers of the Hindu faith.

Devotion or *Bhakti* is something that is nourished and sustained by Faith. While it is true that both faith and devotion are matters of choice, it is also equally true that these two aspects are their own advocates. If you have faith and devotion, you have them regardless of anything!! Sri Krishna, in the Bhagavad Gita, says that devotion is the highest form of spiritual practice. He also says that devotion to God is a sure-shot way to transcend and go beyond the three *gunas* - *sattva (*goodness*), rajas* (passion) and *tamas* (ignorance) - to the state of self-realisation.

Aham Brahmasmi ('I am Brahman' or the 'Supreme Reality', which essentially also means, 'I am Divine') was a *mahakavya* (a great saying) from the Brihadaranyaka Upanishad. God is within each one of us, and it is for us to realise Him. The underlying message of the Vishnu Sahasranama is also an exhortation (even if tacit) to self-realise. Swami Vivekananda, arguably the greatest spokesman in the contemporary times that the Hindu faith has had, while commenting on *Bhakti,* had stated that 'There is *Bhakti* within you, only a veil of lust-and-wealth covers it, and as soon as that is removed *Bhakti* will manifest by itself'.

Beginning with the six questions of King Yudhisthira and ending with a listing of the benefits of chanting and listening to the Vishnu Sahasranama, the entire Sahasranama is replete with shlokas that convey universality and inclusivity. There is the word '*Prajāpatihi*' in the Sahasranama, which means the father or Creator of all creatures. It is a no-brainer that a Creator will only wish and do good for his own 'children' or 'creations'. Similarly, there is the word '*kṛtirātmavān*', meaning He who dwells in each one of us. This again points to inclusivity.

Furthermore, words likc time (*kula*), assumption of many forms *(śatāvartaf)*, establishing of righteousness (*vṛshakarmā),* etc. in the Vishnu Sahasranama denote dynamism, plurality and morality, respectively, amongst many other attributes.

In today's times, where many of us feel that time is at a premium and that the fast-paced life does not allow for taking time out to chant and listening to the Vishnu Sahasranama, Krishna tells Arjuna, in the Bhagavad Gita, that if a devotee were to offer Him a mere leaf, a flower, a fruit or water with sincere devotion and love, He shall accept it as an invaluable treasure. We have already seen that in the Phalashruti (referred to in the Preface of this book), Krishna tells Arjuna that He will be happy if His devotees were to chant even as much as one shloka with sincerity and devotion! Again, Lord Shiva while replying to Parvati's query as to what would be an easy and simple way of chanting the Vishnu Sahasranama says that he himself chants the Rama Nama repeatedly, and 'uttering the Rama Nama **even once** is equivalent to reciting all the thousand *nāmas'*.

There is the Sri Ranganatha Swamy temple in Srirangam in the South Indian state of Tamil Nadu. There is a legend associated with this temple. Sri Ramanuja, who is believed to have lived for 120 years (1017-1137 CE), was a well-read scholar and saint. He was also the chief priest of this temple. It was noticed that one particular devotee would come every day, break the queue for *prasadam* (food that is first offered to a deity and then distributed amongst the devotees in the name of that deity) and leave after collecting more than his own share. When queried, he would say that his family was starving and that he needed more than his share of *prasadam* in order to feed his wife and children.

When this matter was brought to the attention of Sri Ramanuja, he met this devotee and asked him whether he knew the Vishnu Sahasranama, to which the devotee replied that he knew only the first six words, the sixth word being '*bhūtabhṛd*' (One who nurtures and nourishes all beings). Sri Ramanuja asked the devotee to chant this word alone after suffixing '*Namah*' to it ('*bhūtabhṛd namah*') 108 times a day. He further told him that once he did this, he would no longer be required to come to the temple for *prasadam* as he would get all the *prasadam* he required at his home - enough to meet the hunger of his entire family.

Although the devotee left with the promise that he would do as advised, a certain quantity of the temple *prasadam* was found missing every day, even after this. The other devotees suspected that the same man was coming every day to the temple and somehow managed to steal the *prasadam*. They decided to go to his home along with Sri Ramanuja to find out the truth. The devotee seeing Sri Ramanuja profusely thanked him and told him that he was religiously and sincerely following the advice given to him and that a small boy was coming home every day and leaving some *prasadam* in a vessel, satisfying the hunger of everyone in the house. When queried by that devotee as to who the boy was, he replied that he was the servant of Sri Ramanuja and had been instructed to deliver the *prasadam* to his house every day. Sri Ramanuja immediately understood as to who 'his servant' was. Sri Ranganatha (Lord Vishnu) had taken it upon himself to feed the devotee and his family in keeping with his attribute or *nāma* of 'One who nourishes the entire Universe'!

Believers believe that regular chanting of the Vishnu Sahasranama helps to cure grief, confusion, fear and diseases. The Phalashruti says that those afflicted by any of the above have just to call out the name of 'Narayana', and they will not only get rid of all their troubles but also attain everlasting happiness. Sage Vyasa clearly intended the Vishnu Sahasranama to be a panacea not just for everyone but for every situation, too!

I shall end with what Martin Luther, the medieval German theologian, had once said: 'Faith is a living, daring confidence in God's Grace, so sure and certain, that a man could stake his life on it a thousand times'.

Select Bibliography

While writing this book, I benefited immensely from a wide variety of books, websites, podcasts, and discourses by some very eminent and erudite scholars. The list given here is nowhere comprehensive but merely lists the sources which I consulted regularly and frequently:

1. Thousand Ways to the Transcendental: Vishnu Sahasranama by Swami Chinmayananda

2. Vishnu Sahasranama: Acharya Vinobha Bhave

3. Lectures delivered by Shri Dushyant Sridhar at the Bharatiya Vidya Bhavan, Bangalore (https://www.youtube.com/watch?v=oGdQqmKER3A)

4. Sanskrit Channel (https://www.youtube.com/c/thesanskritchannel)

5. Vishnu Sahsranamam (https://www.youtube.com/watch?v=eQoN9_eAJzI): Suresh Gopi

6. Visvas Institute of Shri Vishnu Sahasranama, Chennai

7. 'The Most Powerful Thing You Can Ask God' (https://www.youtube.com/watch?v=69RPRK8oCm4) : Swami Mukundananda of JK Yog; 'The Only Way You Can See Lord Krishna' - An Eye-Opening Video

9 789356 218833

Printed at Repro India Ltd.